M000310066

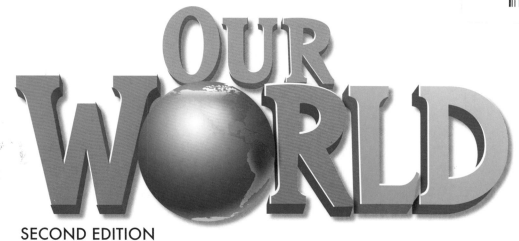

OUR WORLD

SECOND EDITION

Series Editors
Joan Kang Shin and
JoAnn (Jodi) Crandall

Authors
Ronald Scro
and Rob Sved

NATIONAL
GEOGRAPHIC
LEARNING

Australia · Brazil · Mexico · Singapore · United Kingdom · United States

TR: 10.1

This is our world.
Everybody's got a song to sing.
Each boy and girl.
This is our world!
I say "our." You say "world."
Our!
World!
Our!
World!
I say "boy." You say "girl."
Boy!
Girl!

Boy!
Girl!
I say, "Everybody move!"
I say, "Everybody stop!"
Everybody, stop!
This is our world.
Everybody's got a song to sing.
Each boy and girl.
This is our world!

Unit 1 Extreme Weather **6**

Unit 2 Copycat Animals **22**

Unit 3 Music in Our World **38**

Units 1-3 Review **54**

Units 1-3 Extended Reading: Animal Predictions? **56**

Let's Talk! **58**

Unit 4 Life Out There **60**

Unit 5 Arts Lost and Found **76**

Unit 6 Amazing Plants! **92**

Units 4-6 Review **108**

Units 4-6 Extended Reading: Attack of the Extraterrestrial Plants! . **110**

Let's Talk! **112**

Unit 7 Volcanoes **114**

Unit 8 Reduce, Reuse, Recycle **130**

Unit 9 Cool Vacations! **146**

Units 7-9 Review **162**

Units 7-9 Extended Reading: Surviving Krakatoa **164**

Let's Talk! **166**

Irregular Verbs **168**

Cutouts **169**

Stickers

Santorini, Greece

Scope and Sequence

	1 **Extreme Weather** p. 6	2 **Copycat Animals** p. 22	3 **Music in Our World** p. 38	4 **Life Out There** p. 60
CONTENT AREA CONNECTION	Science	Science	Music and the Performing Arts, Visual Arts	Science, Technology and Engineering
GOALS ⏵ SC: 1	• talk about different kinds of extreme weather • describe the damage storms can cause • describe how to prepare for extreme weather • write a personal narrative	• describe animals • compare different animals • talk about how animals imitate others • use classification writing	• talk about different musical instruments and styles • talk about your musical experiences • compare how people make music • do contrast writing	• talk about space and space exploration • talk about different possibilities of life in space • give your opinions about space • do persuasive writing
VOCABULARY 1 & 2 ⏵ SC: 2–4	blizzard, drop, drought, flood, heat wave, hurricane, ice storm, lightning, range, rise, sandstorm, speed, thunder, tornado, tropical storm **Strategy:** Compound nouns emergency, evacuate, flashlight, plan, shelter, supplies **Strategy:** Noun plurals	camouflage, characteristic, copy, frighten, hide, hunt, imitate, insect, poisonous, predator, prey, resemble, species, spot, stripe **Strategy:** Using a dictionary attack, avoid, confuse, defend, escape **Strategy:** Action verbs	band, beat, chord, concert, drum, flute, guitar, lead singer, melody, note, perform, piano, practice, rhythm, saxophone, violin **Strategy:** Multiple-meaning words classical, hip-hop, jazz, pop, rock **Strategy:** Act it out	atmosphere, comet, data, debate, extraterrestrial, galaxy, journey, orbit, planet, solar system, space, the universe **Strategy:** Classification of words astronaut, communicate, rocket, search, spacecraft, space station **Strategy:** Words in context
GRAMMAR 1 & 2 ⏵ SC: 5–6	Future predictions and plans with *be going to* Zero conditional (present tense)	Comparisons with *as . . . as* Tag questions	Present perfect with *ever* and *never* Comparative adverbs	*May* and *might* Indefinite pronouns
READING	Tornado Trouble **Strategy:** Visualize	Copycats **Strategy:** Scan text for information	It's All Music **Strategy:** Ask questions	Listening for Life **Strategy:** Identify the author's purpose
WRITING	**Personal Narrative** Focus: Describe an experience	**Classification Writing** Focus: Show how things belong to a group or category	**Contrast Writing** Focus: Show the differences between things	**Persuasive Writing** Focus: Convince the reader of your opinion
MISSION ⏵ SC: 9	**Understand weather.** **National Geographic Explorer:** Tim Samaras	**Protect biodiversity.** **National Geographic Explorer:** Krithi Karanth	**Change through music.** **National Geographic Awardee:** Jack Johnson	**Live curious.** **National Geographic Explorer:** Kevin Hand
PROJECT	A tornado in a jar	A collage	A musical instrument	Model of life on another planet
REVIEW	**Units 1–3**	pp. 54–55		**Units 4–6**
EXTENDED READING	**Animal Predictions?**	pp. 56–57		**Attack of the Extraterrestrial Plants!**
LET'S TALK	It's my turn. Who's going to take notes?	p. 58 p. 59		Can I borrow your bike? It could work.

⏵ **ADDITIONAL VIDEO** Song: Sc. 7; Viewing: Sc. 8; Storytime: Sc. 10; Wrap Up: Sc. 11

5 Arts Lost and Found p. 76	6 Amazing Plants! p. 92	7 Volcanoes p. 114	8 Reduce, Reuse, Recycle p. 130	9 Cool Vacations! p. 146
The Humanities, Music and the Performing Arts	Science	Science	Science, Visual Arts	Language Arts
• talk about traditions and communities • talk about different craft and cultural activities • understand changing traditions • write a blog entry	• describe plants • talk about what plants and animals do to help plants survive • compare how plants grow and adapt • do descriptive writing	• discuss volcanoes • describe how a volcano erupts • make predictions • write a process description	• discuss the importance of reducing, reusing, and recycling • learn about art from recycled materials • talk about what you can do to help the environment • write a biography	• talk about different vacation places • talk about what you would do in different situations • express preferences • write a review
art, community, culture, future, generation, hold on, language, local, pass down, proud, share, storytelling, tourist, tradition, weave **Strategy:** Using context clues embroidery, handcrafted, jewelry making, pottery, sculpture **Strategy:** Base words	adapt, attract, bacteria, behavior, digest, ground, leaf, light, roots, stem, stink, strategy, survival, trap, trick **Strategy:** Word families daisy, petal, rose, thorn, vine **Strategy:** Contractions	ash, calm, cover, crack, create, deep, erupt, explode, gas, heat, inside, melted, steam, surface, thick, volcano **Strategy:** Multiple-meaning words active, cone, crater, dormant, extinct **Strategy:** Suffixes	build, conserve, design, energy efficient, environment, junk, landfill, man-made, natural, recycle, reduce, renewable, reuse, throw away, trash **Strategy:** Prefix *re-* cardboard, chemicals, glass, metal, tools **Strategy:** Expressing purpose	beach, camping, guide, hike, hotel, photo safari, relax, ruins, tent, theme park, ticket, tour, water park, wildlife **Strategy:** Using a thesaurus airport, passport, souvenir, suitcase, sunglasses **Strategy:** Antonyms and Synonyms
Gerunds as subjects Gerunds as objects	The passive: Simple present Relative clauses with *that*	First conditional *Because of . . .*	Passive with modals (simple present) Clauses with *when*	Second conditional *Would rather*
Not Your Grandpa's Mariachi **Strategy:** Compare and contrast	Is That a Plant? **Strategy:** Use information graphics to support comprehension	Active Volcanoes **Strategy:** Scan text for information	Found Art **Strategy:** Understand the author's purpose	Tree House Vacation **Strategy:** Use visuals to support comprehension
Blog Entry **Focus:** Write about your thoughts	**Descriptive Writing** **Focus:** Describe what something looks like and what it does	**Process Description** **Focus:** Explain what happens in a sequence	**Biography** **Focus:** Write about the life and work of a person	**Travel Review** **Focus:** Write about a vacation experience
Value your cultural traditions. **National Geographic Explorer:** Dr. Elizabeth Kapu'uwailani Lindsey	**Value plants.** **National Geographic Explorer:** Maria Fadiman	**Help in a disaster.** **National Geographic Explorer:** Patrick Meier	**Help reduce our human footprint.** **National Geographic Explorer:** Alexandra Cousteau	**Be a respectful tourist.** **National Geographic Explorer:** Joseph Lekuton
Museum of the future	Local plant guide	A volcano	Recycled art	A tourist brochure
pp. 108–109		**Units 7–9**	pp. 162–163	
pp. 110–111		**Surviving Krakatoa**	pp. 164–165	
p. 112 p. 113		**No way!** **Our presentation is about . . .**	p. 166 p. 167	

Extreme Weather

In this unit, I will . . .
- talk about different kinds of extreme weather.
- describe the damage storms can cause.
- describe how to prepare for extreme weather.
- write a personal narrative.

Check T for *True* and F for *False*.

1. There's a storm cloud in the sky.   **T**   **F**

2. The trees are covered in ice.   **T**   **F**

3. It's raining heavily.   **T**   **F**

4. It's safe to be outside.   **T**   **F**

Supercell thunderstorm,
Colorado, USA

1 **Listen and read.** TR: 1.1

2 **Listen and repeat.** TR: 1.2

We know we can't control the weather. It can be beautiful, wild, and dangerous, often all at the same time. Scientists try to predict weather in different ways. They tell us when extreme weather is coming. Then we can try to protect ourselves.

Thunderstorms bring heavy rain with loud **thunder** and **lightning**. If too much rain falls in a short time, it can cause a **flood**. Too little rain makes the land dry and can cause a **drought**. When it's very cold, a rainstorm can turn into an **ice storm** or a **blizzard**.

lightning

Grand Canyon, USA

a hurricane

a sandstorm

Wind is a dangerous force. In a **tropical storm**, the wind **speed** can be more than 100 kilometers (60 miles) per hour. Wind in a **hurricane**, or cyclone, is even faster.

High winds in dry places such as deserts can pick up sand and cause a **sandstorm**. A **tornado** is a column of wind that rotates very fast.

We can only live within a specific **range** of temperatures. At times, temperatures **rise** too high or **drop** too low. It not only feels bad, it can be dangerous! In a **heat wave**, the weather stays very hot for days or even weeks.

3 **Ask and answer.**
Work with a partner.
What did you learn?

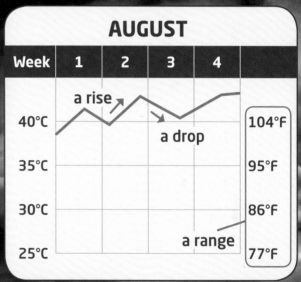

AUGUST				
Week	1	2	3	4

a rise
a drop
a range

40°C — 104°F
35°C — 95°F
30°C — 86°F
25°C — 77°F

Yes, it can. It can cause a heatwave.

When the weather is hot, can it be dangerous?

1 **Listen, read, and sing.** TR: 1.3

Bad Weather

There's bad weather on the way!
There's bad weather on the way!

Is it going to storm? Yes, it is!
Is there going to be lightning? Yes, there is!
Is there going to be thunder? Yes, there is!

When there's going to be a storm, I hurry inside!

CHORUS
Be prepared for emergencies.
It's always good to be safe. You'll see!
Grab supplies and a flashlight, too.
Seek shelter. It's the safe thing to do!

Is there going to be a blizzard? Yes, there is!
Is there going to be an ice storm? Yes, there is!
Is it going to be cold? Oh, yes it is!
If there's going to be a blizzard, I hurry inside!

CHORUS

Is there going to be a hurricane? Yes, there is!
Is the wind going to howl? Yes, it is!
Are the waves going to rage? Yes, they are!

If there's going to be a hurricane, we evacuate!

CHORUS
Seek shelter. It's the safe thing to do!

2 **Ask and answer.** Work with a partner.

1. What bad storm in your town do you remember?
2. What did you do to prepare?
3. What did you think and feel during the storm?

The Netherlands

GRAMMAR 1

Future predictions and plans with *be going to* TR: 1.4

Is it **going to** rain tomorrow? No, it**'s going to** snow tomorrow.
I**'m going to** listen to the weather report at 8:00.
He**'s going to** put on his snow boots.

1 **Write.** What is the weather going to be like?

Monday   Tuesday

Wednesday   Thursday   Friday

1. It's going to rain on Monday. _____

2. _____

3. _____

4. _____

5. _____

2 **Ask and answer.** Read. Take turns.

1. Why can't we go to the park tomorrow? (rain)
2. Won't she get wet walking in the rain? (take an umbrella)
3. Why is she closing the windows? (rain)
4. When is he going to get a new raincoat? (today)

3 **Write.** What are you going to do?

A thunderstorm is coming. _____

_____

_____

_____

A heat wave is coming. _____

_____

_____

_____

A hurricane is coming. _____

_____

_____

_____

4 **Ask and answer.** Work with a partner. What about you? Talk about today and tomorrow.

A blizzard is coming.

That's right. It's going to snow a lot. Let's play inside.

13

VOCABULARY 2

1 **Listen and repeat.** Then read and write. TR: 1.5

a plan

evacuate

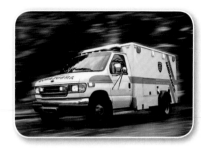

an emergency

a flashlight

supplies

a shelter

When a weather forecaster predicts bad weather, you can make a

_____ to prepare. To protect yourself from wind and

rain, you should go to a _____. If the electricity goes

off, use a _____ to see in the dark. You can store

_____ in a safe place so that you have food to eat.

A really bad storm can affect the whole town. In an _____

like that, people have to _____ and go where it's safer.

2 **Listen and stick.** Find out what to do next. Place your stickers in the correct order. Work with a partner.
Summarize the weather report. TR: 1.6

> A hurricane is coming. It's an emergency.

> Yes, I put a plan in number 1. That's correct.

1 **2** **3** **4** **5**

GRAMMAR 2

Zero conditional (present tense) TR: 1.7

I **put on** my winter coat **if** the weather **is** cold.
If I **see** lightning, I **go** inside.
If a sandstorm **comes,** I **close** all the windows.

1 **Match and make logical sentences.** What do you do in these situations? Write five sentences of your own in your notebook.

If I see lightning when I'm swimming,	I look for a boat.
If it rains,	I wear gloves and boots.
If a storm comes,	I try to stay cool.
If the temperature rises,	I get out of the water.
If a flood comes,	I go inside the house.
If it snows,	I use an umbrella.

2 **Play a game.** Cut out the cards in the back of the book. Play with a partner. Take turns. Match and make sentences. Keep the cards.

If it rains, I use an umbrella.

1 **Listen and read.** TR: 1.8

Tornado *Trouble*

Tornadoes happen all over the world. There's even a place called Tornado Alley. Josh Wurman studies extreme weather. He joined a team of other scientists to study tornadoes in Tornado Alley. One day, the blue sky turned black. A giant cloud came toward the team. The cloud had winds that moved in a circle. Inside his truck, Wurman watched the storm through his window and on his instruments. Colors on the computer screen showed where the rain fell and where the wind was the strongest.

The winds twisted the storm tighter and tighter into the shape of a funnel. When the funnel touched the ground, it became a tornado! The tornado looked like a giant, gray elephant's trunk. It moved one way, then another way. As the tornado moved across the ground, the team came dangerously close. They dropped special instruments close to the storm. These instruments showed wind speed, temperature, and how much rain was falling.

The tornado twisted and moved for half an hour. The team watched the storm and their instruments the whole time. Then the tornado leaned over slowly like a soft rope. Poof! It was gone. The excitement was over. But Wurman and his team have a lot more work to do. The information from their instruments will help them predict other tornadoes so that they can warn people and save lives.

It once rained frogs on a town in Serbia. A small tornado dropped them there.

2 Discuss. Work in groups of three. Answer the questions.

1. What is the shape of a tornado?
2. Where does a funnel touch to become a tornado?
3. Why do scientists study tornadoes?
4. What do scientists use to learn about tornadoes?

3 Match. Work with a partner. How does a tornado form?
Match the text to each step. Discuss.

a. Warm and cold air currents twist winds into a funnel. Then the funnel touches the ground.
b. Warm air and cold air come together. They make a twisting wind of air that moves in circles.
c. The twisting air stands up. Warm air moves up. Cold air moves down.

 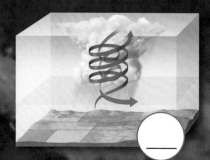 

4 Work with a group. Compare tornadoes and hurricanes. Discuss. Complete the chart.

Tornado	Hurricane
	Origin: They form over water. Duration: They last a week.

Dodge City, Kansas, USA

WRITING

Personal Narrative When you write a personal narrative, you tell a story. You want the reader to feel like he or she is there. To do this, you can use descriptive language that uses the senses—sight, sound, taste, smell, and touch. To express the sequence of events, you can use time expressions such as *after, before, next,* and *then.*

1 **Read.** Read the personal narrative. How does the writer describe the hurricane? How does the writer describe what she hears and sees? How does she feel? Circle the words that relate to the senses and emotions. Underline the words and expressions that show the sequence of events.

Safe not Sorry!

If a hurricane comes, we know what to do. We have a family plan.

Last year, the weather forecaster told us that a hurricane was coming. First, I helped my dad put heavy wood over the windows. It was hard work. Next, we went inside the house and turned on the radio to listen for news about the hurricane. When the hurricane came, we could hear the strong winds outside. It was scary. The rain came down hard on the roof, too. Then suddenly, there was a loud crash. The whole house shook! Everyone was worried. What was it? Soon, it was quiet and we could go outside. We saw a huge tree on the ground. Part of the tree hit the wood on the window.

I am *so* happy we had a family plan! Hopefully, there isn't going to be a hurricane for a while.

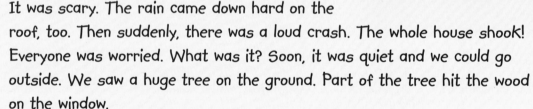

2 **Write.** Write about an extreme weather experience. Give details relating to the senses. Help the reader feel what you felt.

3 **Share.** Share your writing. Work in a small group. Listen and take notes.

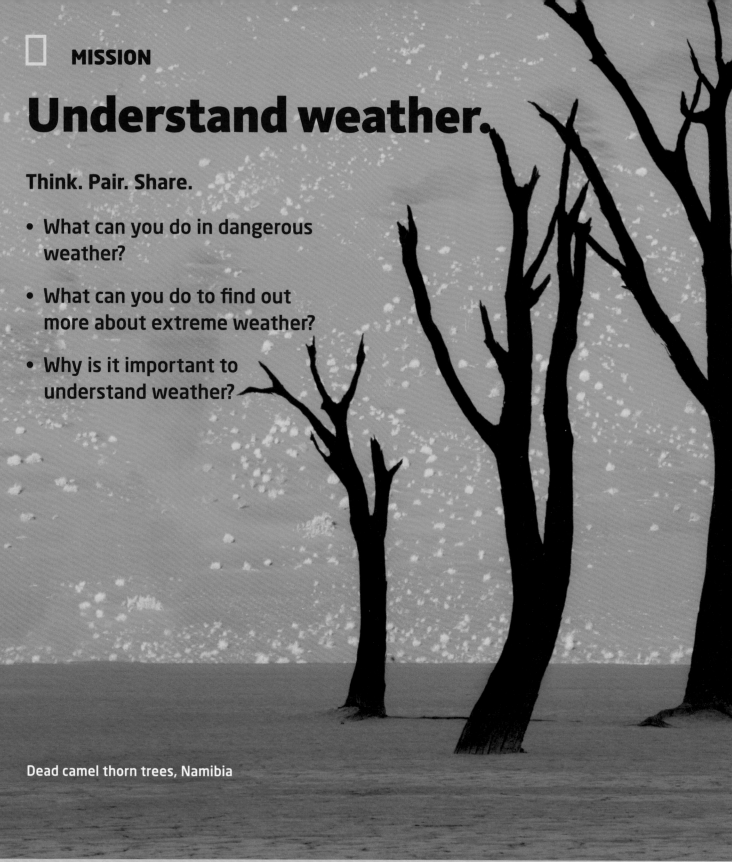

Understand weather.

Think. Pair. Share.

- What can you do in dangerous weather?

- What can you do to find out more about extreme weather?

- Why is it important to understand weather?

Dead camel thorn trees, Namibia

"It all started when I was about six years old and saw that fantastic tornado in *The Wizard of Oz.***"**

Tim Samaras (1957–2013), Severe Storm Researcher,
National Geographic Explorer

PROJECT

Make your own tornado.

1 Work in small groups to make a tornado in a bottle.

2 You need a glass jar or bottle, some water, some dishwashing liquid, and some glitter.

3 Pour water into the bottle, about three-quarters full. Then add a small amount of dishwashing liquid.

4 Add a little glitter.

5 Put on the lid tightly.

6 Then, shake the bottle around in a circle and watch your tornado!

If I shake the jar around, the glitter looks like a tornado.

Now I can . . .

○ talk about different kinds of extreme weather.

○ describe the damage storms can cause.

○ describe how to prepare for extreme weather.

○ write a personal narrative.

Copycat Animals

In this unit, I will . . .
- describe animals.
- compare different animals.
- talk about how animals imitate others.
- use classification writing.

Check T for *True* and F for *False*.

1. This is a plant.   (T) (F)

2. It is very soft.   (T) (F)

3. It is very small.   (T) (F)

4. It has sharp teeth.   (T) (F)

Allied cowrie,
Papua New Guinea

VOCABULARY 1

1 **Listen and read.** TR: 2.1

2 **Listen and repeat.** TR: 2.2

Some animals can look like other animals or even like a plant! These copycats are trying to hide from or trick a hungry **predator**. They can look like another more dangerous animal or like another animal the predator doesn't like to eat.

This cheetah's black **spots** act as **camouflage**. This way, the cheetah doesn't **frighten** its **prey** when it's time to **hunt**.

spots

a predator

a stripe

This colorful frog has **stripes** on its skin. The bright colors tell hungry predators that the frog is **poisonous**.

These butterflies are not the same **species**, but they **resemble** each other. The top one tastes bad. The other one **copies** its shape and colors, and tastes bad, too.

prey

This **insect** is as green as a leaf. It **imitates** the **characteristics** of color and shape of leaves to help it **hide** from predators.

3 **Ask and answer.** Work with a partner. What did you learn?

How do some frogs show they are poisonous?

They have bright colors.

25

1 **Listen, read, and sing.** TR: 2.3

It's a Wild World

CHORUS

It's a wild world!
It's work to stay alive!
Animals do amazing things
in order to survive.

An insect that looks like a leaf
copies plants to get relief.
Predators are everywhere,
and looking for a feast!

CHORUS

Camouflage and imitate.
Resemble and escape!
Animals hide in front of our eyes, every day.

The hunter and the hunted,
predator and prey,
must hunt or hide to stay alive,
each and every day.

A pretty frog can be as deadly as a snake.
Its stripes tell its enemies
"You'd better stay away!"

CHORUS

It's a wild world!

2 **Ask and answer.** Work with a partner.

1. What predators have you seen?
2. What is their prey?
3. How does the prey avoid predators?

Stonefish,
Red Sea, Egypt

GRAMMAR 1

Comparisons with *as . . . as* TR: 2.4

That katydid is **as** green **as** the leaf it sits on.
That butterfly is **not as** pretty **as** the blue one.
Poison dart frogs are **as** dangerous **as** some snakes.

1 **Read and write.** Work with a partner. Take turns. Compare.

1. some insects / thin / sticks

_____

2. a polar bear / white / snow

_____

3. king snakes / not dangerous / coral snakes

_____

4. a bee sting / bad / a wasp sting

_____

5. a lion / not loud / a howler monkey

_____

a bee

a wasp

2 **Compare the animals.** Work with a partner. Choose one word from each group. Make sentences.

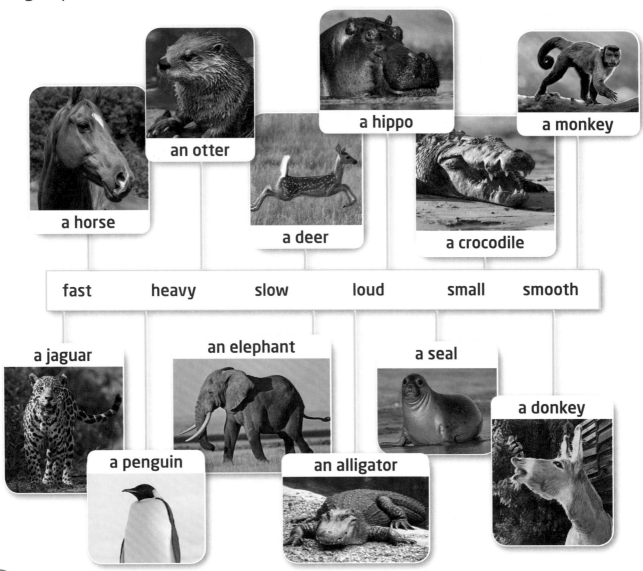

a horse · an otter · a hippo · a monkey · a deer · a crocodile

fast · heavy · slow · loud · small · smooth

a jaguar · an elephant · a seal · a penguin · an alligator · a donkey

3 **Make sentences.** Work in a group. Take turns. Use the last word in each sentence to start the next sentence.

The hippo is as big as the car.

The car is as green as the frog.

The frog is as funny as you are. Ha ha!

VOCABULARY 2

1 **Listen and repeat.** Then read and write. TR: 2.5

The butterfly fish **confuses** its predators with a spot like an eye.

Jaguars **attack** their prey.

The cobra **defends** itself. The mongoose **avoids** its bite.

Deer **escape** predators by running away.

1. All predators _____ prey.

2. Bluebirds _____ their eggs from predators.

3. Calabar pythons have tails that look like heads. This _____

   predators so they will not know where to strike!

4. Some animals use camouflage to _____ predators.

5. A rabbit that runs fast can _____ the coyote

   that chases it.

2 **Listen.** Stick True or False. Work with a partner.
Compare your answers. TR: 2.6

> The spot on the tail looks like an eye.
> The sentence is true.

>> You are right! My turn.

1   2   3   4   5

GRAMMAR 2

Tag questions TR: 2.7

The jaguar **is** dangerous, **isn't it?**
Those snakes **are** scary, **aren't they?**
This insect **looks** like a stick, **doesn't it?**
Giraffes **don't** eat meat, **do they?**

That frog **wasn't** poisonous, **was it?**
The cat **escaped** the dog, **didn't it?**
The dogs **were** loud, **weren't they?**
The cats **weren't** friendly, **were they?**

1 **Read.** Complete the sentences.

1. The katydid is pretending it's a leaf, _____?

2. The donkey doesn't look thirsty, _____?

3. That python really confused its predator, _____?

4. Cats like sleeping in the sun, _____?

5. Baby penguins are so cute, _____?

6. Those weren't copycat animals, _____?

2 **Play a game.** Cut out the question tags in the back of the book. Glue nine to complete your game. Listen. Which tag completes the sentence? If you have it, draw an X on the square. TR: 2.8

I have three in a row!

31

1 **Listen and read.** TR: 2.9

One kind of spider tricks predators by imitating an ant. It holds two legs up to look more like an ant when it walks.

COPYcats

The leafy sea dragon is a weird but beautiful copycat. From its name you would think it imitates a dragon, wouldn't you? But no, it only gets that name from its funny shape. The leafy sea dragon imitates what is around it. It lives in seaweed, and so its body looks like a seaweed leaf. The sea dragon imitates the shape and color of seaweed, and it even looks like floating seaweed when it moves. It doesn't use the parts of its body that look like a leaf to swim. It uses fins that are transparent, so it's hard to see them move.

The leafy sea dragon does not only look like a copycat. It also dances like a copycat. A male and female sea dragon will copy each other's movements for hours!

The mimic octopus is the only sea creature that can imitate many different species. It not only changes its color, it also changes its shape. It has arms as thick as pencils. When it spreads them wide, they look like the spines of a lionfish. It hides some of its arms in the sand but leaves two arms out. Then with its white and brown stripes and the two arms, it looks like a sea snake! It can also pull its arms together and swim on the sea floor, so to a predator, it looks like a poisonous flatfish!

Like other octopuses, the mimic octopus has eight arms and three hearts. It swims by shooting out jets of water through a siphon. It also has a large brain for its size. That's one smart octopus!

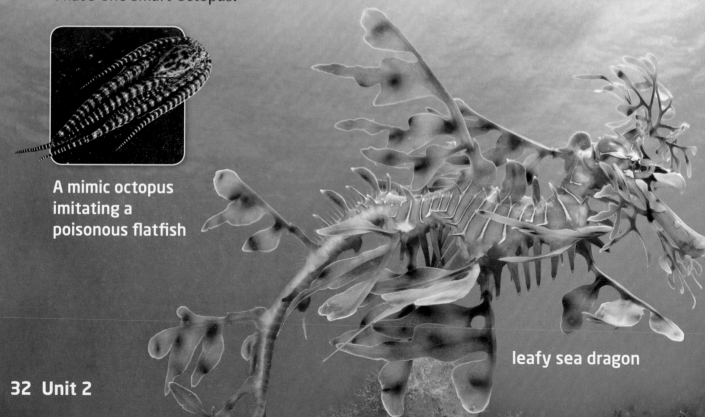

A mimic octopus imitating a poisonous flatfish

leafy sea dragon

2 Read and write. Work with a partner. Compare your answers.

1. What does the leafy sea dragon imitate?

   _____

2. What does the leafy sea dragon use to swim?

   _____

3. What does the mimic octopus look like?

   _____

4. What does the mimic octopus do with its arms?

   _____

3 Work with a partner. Choose the leafy sea dragon or the mimic octopus to talk about. Your partner will listen and complete the first row. Then listen to your partner and fill in the second row.

an octopus

Habitat	Shape	Color	Movement

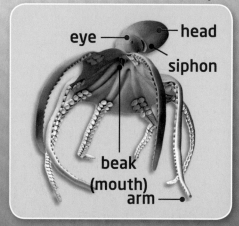

eye — head
siphon
beak (mouth)
arm —

4 Summarize the reading. Work in groups of three. Take turns.

The leafy sea dragon is a copycat animal.

But it doesn't look like a dragon.

Yeah, it looks like seaweed.

WRITING

Classification Writing You can organize your writing by placing information into categories or groups. You can define, compare, and contrast details to show how things belong to a category or group. You can use words such as *both, like, but,* and *unlike.*

1 **Read.** Read about two types of copycat animals. How does the writer classify them? What words does the writer use to show that the animals are similar or different? Underline the words and expressions.

Animals That Imitate

Some animals copy other animals to avoid attack. Some species copy the appearance or the sound of another animal.

The monarch butterfly is poisonous to many predators. The viceroy butterfly is also poisonous and it looks like the monarch butterfly. So predators don't eat it. Like the viceroy butterfly, the ash borer moth changes its appearance to protect itself. It doesn't have a stinger, but it looks like a wasp so predators avoid it.

Other species copy the sound of another animal. When termites feed under the leaves, they make a hissing sound, like a snake. A dormouse does the same thing. When it is in a dark hole, it hisses loudly. Predators leave both of these animals alone!

viceroy butterfly

ash borer moth

2 **Write.** Write about animals that belong to a certain category. Describe the characteristics that they share and the characteristics that are different.

3 **Share.** Share your writing. Work in a small group. Listen and take notes.

Protect biodiversity.

Think. Pair. Share.

- Think about your community. How does biodiversity affect it?

- What can you do to find out more about local species?

- Why is it important to preserve diverse species?

A Bengal tiger,
Bandhavgarh National Park, India

"We need to increase people's interest and support for wildlife and wild places, particularly children who are stewards of the future of nature."

Krithi Karanth, Conservation Biologist, National Geographic Explorer

PROJECT

Make a collage.

1 Work in small groups. Choose a habitat such as an ocean, a forest, or a desert.

2 Discuss how animals protect themselves in that place.

3 In your part of the collage, show some animals that use camouflage and some that survive in other ways.

There is a leaf-tailed gecko on a tree trunk in the rain forest. It uses camouflage to survive. Can you see it?

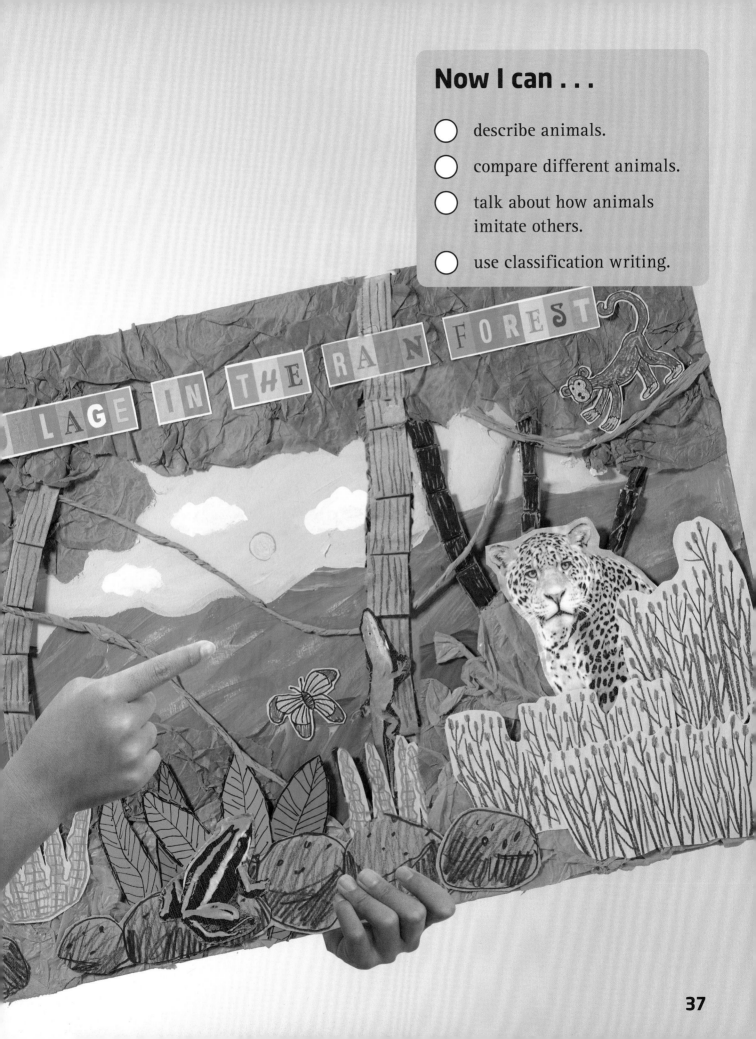

Now I can . . .

- ○ describe animals.
- ○ compare different animals.
- ○ talk about how animals imitate others.
- ○ use classification writing.

Music
in Our World

In this unit, I will . . .
- talk about different musical instruments and styles.
- talk about my musical experiences.
- compare how people make music.
- do contrast writing.

Circle the correct answer.

1. The man is using

    a. a hunting tool.

    b. a musical instrument.

2. He is playing

    a. traditional music.

    b. classical music.

Makena Beach, Maui

VOCABULARY 1

1 **Listen and read.** TR: 3.1

2 **Listen and repeat.** TR: 3.2

There are three main types of musical instruments. String instruments make sounds when you pluck the strings. Wind instruments make sounds when you blow air through them. Percussion instruments make different sounds when you hit them or shake them.

Music has its own language. Each single sound is a **note**. Play two notes or more at one time to make a **chord**. Notes and chords played one after the other make a **melody**. The thump, thump, thump that makes you want to dance is the **beat**. Put all the beats together, slow and fast, repeat them over time, and you have a **rhythm**.

a violin

a drum

a piano

a flute

a saxophone

a guitar

Sleepy Man Banjo Boys,
Indio, California

Do you want your **band** to play better? You have to **practice!** Play songs again and again until they sound really good. When your band sounds good, you can **perform** for an audience. Invite your friends to the **concert!** If you don't play an instrument but you sing well, you could be the **lead singer!**

3 **Ask and answer.** Work with a partner. What did you learn?

How many types of instruments are there?

There are three main types.

1 **Listen, read, and sing.** TR: 3.3

Music Is Fun

CHORUS
Have you ever listened to hip-hop?
Have you ever listened to drums?
I listen to all kinds of music.
It's amazing fun.

Listen to the saxophone.
Listen to the beat.
Listen to the melody.
Feel it in your feet!

The flute is playing.
The piano is, too.
I can hear the guitar.
Can you?

CHORUS

Listen to the rhythm.
Listen to that band!
Sing the notes (la la la)
and clap your hands.

Have you ever played a note?
Have you ever played a chord?
Have you ever played a rhythm:
1, 2, 3, 4?

CHORUS

2 **Ask and answer.** Work with a partner.

1. Who are your favorite musicians?
2. What instruments do they play?
3. Why do you like their music?

Pantsula, Alexandra, South Africa

GRAMMAR 1

Present perfect with *ever* and *never* TR: 3.4

Have you **ever listened** to hip-hop?
Have you **ever danced** to hip-hop?
Have you **ever been** to a concert?
Has Lisa **ever heard** an orchestra perform?

Yes, I **have**.
No, I **haven't**.
No, I **never have**.
No, she **has never heard** an orchestra perform.

1 **Read.** Complete the sentences.

1. This song is new. I ___have never heard___ (hear) it before.

2. I _____ (go) to see an opera. I don't think I'd like it.

3. _____ (listen) to jazz? Yes, I like it!

4. If you _____ (hear) her sing, then you know she

   sings well.

5. This is his first time. He _____ (perform)

   in public.

6. _____ you _____ (dance) to a slow song?

Chinese opera

2 **Write.** What about you? Write questions. Work with a partner. Answer each other's questions.

1. go / rock concert ___Have you ever gone to a rock concert?___

2. play / a musical instrument _____

3. take / music lessons _____

4. watch / a band _____

5. listen to / classical music _____

6. sing / in public _____

7. hear / your brother sing _____

8. perform / in public _____

3 **Ask and answer.** Work in groups of three. Use words from the list. Take turns.

band	guitar	dance	play
concert	piano	have jazz lessons	sing
drums	saxophone	listen to	take
famous	singer	meet	watch

Have you ever listened to your sister sing?

Of course I've listened to her sing. She's OK, I guess.

45

VOCABULARY 2

1 **Listen and repeat.** Then read and write. TR: 3.5

hip-hop

classical

pop

jazz

rock

1. A large orchestra that includes cellos, violins, and trumpets often plays

   _____ music.

2. Some music uses spoken words instead of singing. It's called _____.

3. A type of music with swing and rhythm that began 100 years ago and had

   links to the music of West Africa is _____.

4. This music is made for many, many people to enjoy. It's easy to listen to.

   It's _____ music.

5. This music has a strong beat and fast rhythm. It's called _____.

2 **Talk and stick.** Work with a partner. Rank the types of music
(1 = most favorite). Discuss your favorite music and give examples
of songs and performers.

1   2   3   4   5

GRAMMAR 2

> **Comparative adverbs** TR: 3.6
>
> He sings **more loudly than** I do.   She plays the violin **better than** he does.
> I play the guitar **as well as** my brother.   He practices piano **less often than** I do.

1 **Read and write.** Make comparisons. Use five words from the list.

> beautifully   fast   hard   often   slow   well   worse

1. He's good. He plays guitar _____ he plays the drums.

2. That's not good. The orchestra sounds _____ the band.

3. She practices _____ than he does. She plays at least

   twice a day.

4. I dance to hip-hop _____ I dance to rock.

5. I play the piano _____ my older sister.

2 **Play a game.** Play with a partner. Take turns. Spin and make sentences with a comparison.

My sister sings better than I do.

1 **Listen and read.** TR: 3.7

It's *All Music*

People made music before they could write about it. One of the oldest instruments ever found is more than 42,000 years old. It's a flute. Instruments like flutes are called *wind instruments*. The music comes from moving air, usually when a person blows into the instrument. Each wind instrument has a shape that makes its sound different. Some have holes for fingers to cover. Others have buttons to press. Holes and buttons let you change the way the air travels to change the notes.

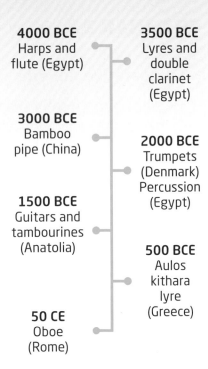

4000 BCE
Harps and flute (Egypt)

3500 BCE
Lyres and double clarinet (Egypt)

3000 BCE
Bamboo pipe (China)

2000 BCE
Trumpets (Denmark) Percussion (Egypt)

1500 BCE
Guitars and tambourines (Anatolia)

500 BCE
Aulos kithara lyre (Greece)

50 CE
Oboe (Rome)

Another way to make music is with strings. When you pluck a string, it makes a note. String instruments have thick or thin strings and long or short strings to make different notes. The shape of the stringed instrument also helps to make the sound. If the shape is bigger, the music sounds lower. Musicians often use a bow to play string instruments. The bow is a piece of wood with hairs or a string stretched between its ends. Musicians slide it over the strings to make sounds.

You can also make music by hitting or shaking something. Percussion instruments can be made from many things. That's because most things make a sound when you hit them. The air inside the instrument makes the sound louder. A drum is a percussion instrument, but instruments with strings can be percussion instruments, too. When you hit strings, you can make music. A piano is a percussion instrument. When you press the piano keys, hammers inside the piano hit the strings to make music.

Varanasi, Uttar Pradesh State, India

2 Choose the best answer.

1. A drum is a _____.

   a. string instrument   b. percussion instrument   c. wind instrument

2. If you press a button on a wind instrument, the sound changes because _____.

   a. your finger is heavy

   b. it holds the instrument tightly

   c. the path of the air changes

3. An empty space inside percussion instruments makes the sound _____.

   a. softer   b. faster   c. louder

4. Some string instruments are played with a _____.

   a. bow   b. hammer   c. key

3 Match the instruments and their types. Work with a partner. Check the correct column.

	Wind	String	Percussion
Drums			
Flute			
Guitar			
Piano			
Saxophone			
Violin			

Mozart composed his first song when he was five years old.

4 Work in groups of three. Invent a unique band that mixes different musical instruments. What six instruments would you choose?

WRITING

Contrast Writing When you contrast things, you show the differences between them. You can use facts and descriptive details to contrast different characteristics. You can also use words like *but*, *although*, *unlike*, *while*, *instead*, and *in contrast* to show things that are not the same.

1 **Read.** Read the text about two ways to compose music. How does the writer show they are different? Underline the words used.

Composing, Then and Now

In the past, composers wrote down their music with paper and a pen. They wrote short lines and dots. This showed another person how to play the music. They couldn't record the music, so people always played the music to each other. But now, technology has changed all this.

For about 150 years, people have recorded music electronically. Today computers are helping people to write music more easily. While in the past composers had to write on paper, today computers can do that for them. A person sings a melody, and then the computer writes the notes!

Before, when composers wanted to make changes, they had to stop and erase the notes. Instead, composers today can touch a screen a few times and make big changes to their music. While a traditional composer was busy cleaning ink off his fingers, a modern composer writes more songs instead!

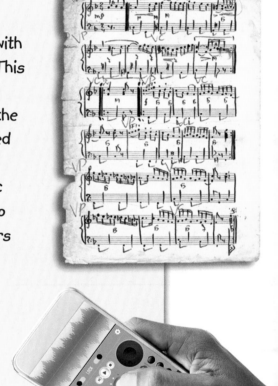

2 **Write.** Write about two styles of music or two musical instruments. How are they different? Use words and expressions that show contrast.

3 **Share.** Share your writing. Work in a small group. Listen and take notes.

Change through music.

Think. Pair. Share.

- How does music change how you think and feel?

- Think of a song. How has it changed how you think?

- How can music make the world a better place?

"Music can change the world. It can inspire people to care, to do something positive, to make a difference."

Jack Johnson, Artist and National Geographic Awardee

PROJECT

Make an instrument.

1 Work in small groups and research homemade musical instruments.

2 Collect trash and junk to make a musical instrument.

3 Join other groups with instruments and practice.

4 Have a concert!

We made percussion and wind instruments. They sound awesome!

Now I can . . .

○ talk about different musical instruments and styles.

○ talk about my musical experiences.

○ compare how people make music.

○ do contrast writing.

Review

1 **Listen and write.** Carla is doing a survey about music. What are her questions? What do Laura and Andres answer? Complete the chart. TR: 3.8

Questions	Laura	Andres
1.	hip-hop	
2.		
3.		He likes to sing. He sang in public once.
4.	none	

2 **Do a survey.** Ask two other students the same questions. Take notes.

3 **Ask and answer.** Work in groups of three. One of you is going on vacation to a place with extreme weather. How are you going to prepare? Take turns to ask questions and give advice.

hurricane
sandstorm
flood
ice storm
heat wave
ever
blizzard
never
tornado
plan
tropical storm

I'm going to Antarctica! That's cool, isn't it? Have you ever been there?

No, I've never been there. What are you going to pack?

I'm going to bring very warm gloves!

If you go to Antarctica, you need more than warm gloves!

4 **Match the copycat animal.** Find the photo that matches the text.

 gecko

 mantid

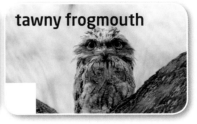 tawny frogmouth

1. This animal's skin is as rough as a tree. It is brown like a tree, too! That helps it hide from predators.

2. This animal has feathers as brown as the color of wood. If it hears you, it doesn't move. It makes its body stiff. It looks just like a tree branch!

3. This animal imitates the color of a dead leaf. It uses the leaf as camouflage. Even if you look for it, you will never see it!

5 **Write.** Continue the story. Work in groups of four. Choose a story. Read it aloud. Then add your own sentence to the story. Take turns. Then share your story with another group.

1

It is raining hard. Paolo runs under a tree. Maria is already standing there, too. They can hear thunder. Then there is a flash of lightning! Maria says …

2

A few friends met to play music. Paolo is good at playing guitar. Maria has a pretty voice. Alba has a drum. They talk about what music to play.

_____

_____

_____

_____

1 Listen and read. TR: 3.9

Animal *Predictions?*

Have you ever heard that animals can sense weather? Many people tell stories about this, but is this true? Some scientists say that it might be. We're going to look at a few examples.

Many people who have dogs know about their behavior. They can see when dogs are more nervous than usual. One example is Champ, an 11-year-old dog who went down to the basement and wouldn't come out. His family knew he was scared. They looked at the sky and saw a tornado coming. So they took shelter in the basement, too. The tornado destroyed their house but they were safe in the basement with Champ. Dogs can hear low sounds, feel changes in air pressure, and smell better than people. So they can often help tell when a storm is coming.

Birds often change their movements before a storm. Golden winged warblers are birds that migrate from Latin America to North America. In 2014, scientists studying migration noticed that the birds weren't in the state of Tennessee at the right time. In fact, they flew 1,500 kilometers (900 miles) more to avoid a huge storm. It is possible they heard the low sounds from the thunder. They returned to Tennessee a few days later.

Have you ever heard that some species can predict earthquakes and tsunamis? Elephants are very good at this. Their big feet can feel vibrations in the ground. In the 2004 tsunami in Thailand, elephants escaped up the hills before the sea water flooded the beaches. They probably felt early vibrations of the earthquake that caused the tsunami.

With time, we will understand more about animals and how they react. The next time the weather forecast says a storm is coming, watch the animals around you. Are they predicting it, too?

Nebraska, USA

2 Read. Check T for *True* and F for *False*.

1. We know a lot about elephants because many people live with them. (T) (F)

2. Scientists were studying bird migration when they discovered that the birds predicted the weather. (T) (F)

3. Champ, the dog, wasn't disturbed by the storm. (T) (F)

4. Storms can make low sounds that humans can't hear. (T) (F)

3 Read. What helps these animals predict storms? Work with a partner and complete the table.

Dog	Bird	Elephant

4 Express yourself. Choose an activity.

1. Pretend you are a scientist observing one of the animals in the text. Write down your observations.

2. What other stories have you heard of animals sensing storms or other weather events? Write a short paragraph about it.

3. How do *you* know the weather is changing? Can you think of signs? Complete the table and then discuss with a partner.

Tornado	Hurricane	Earthquake	Tsunami

Let's Talk

It's my turn.

I will . . .
- take turns.
- give commands.
- talk about who won a game.

1 **Listen and read.** TR: 3.10

Marco: **Whose turn is it?**
Amy: It's my turn.
Marco: Well, **hurry up!**

Amy: **Yay, I won!**
Marco: Now **we're tied.**
Amy: **No way.** What do you mean?
Marco: Well, I won last time!

Whose turn is it? It's my turn. It's his / her turn.	Hurry up! Come on!	Yay! **I won!** **We're tied.** Sorry, you lost!	No way. That's not true. That's not possible.

2 **Discuss.** Work with a partner. Use the chart. Take turns to talk about playing a game.

Who's going to take notes?

I will . . .
• talk about a classroom task.
• make a request.
• offer to do something.

3 **Listen and read.** TR: 3.11

Sonia: So, I'll be the reporter. **Who's going to** take notes?

Olga: **I'll do that.**

Sonia: Thanks. **Can you** watch the time, Hans?

Hans: Sure.

Hans: Um, **what page are we on?**

Olga: **We're on page** 25. We're sharing ideas about music.

Hans: Thanks, Olga.

Who's going to _____ ? Can you _____ ?	I'll do that. I'll (watch the time). I'll be _____ . I can _____ .	What page are we on? Which page is it?	We're on page _____ .
		How long do we have?	We have _____ .
		What are we doing?	We're _____ .

4 **Listen to two discussions.** Circle what the students are doing. TR: 3.12

1. They're **doing a role play / preparing a poster**. Olga is going to
   do the art / write.

2. They're doing a **role play / crossword**. Olga's going to watch the **time /class**.

5 **Discuss.** Work in groups of three. Prepare and practice discussions. Choose one task. Discuss how you are going to do it.

1. Make a musical instrument from recycled objects.

2. Make a mural about copycat animals.

3. Make a poster about the weather.

Unit 4

Life Out There

In this unit, I will . . .
* talk about space and space exploration.
* talk about different possibilities of life in space.
* give my opinions about space.
* do persuasive writing.

Circle the correct letter or write.

1. What do you see in the sky?

   a. clouds   b. stars

2. What time of the day is it?

   a. the afternoon   b. the evening

3. Imagine you are there. Describe what you might see and hear:

   _____

The Milky Way,
Mojave Desert, USA

VOCABULARY 1

1 **Listen and read.** TR: 4.1

2 **Listen and repeat.** TR: 4.2

Earth is a **planet** that moves around the sun. Other planets also **orbit** the sun. The sun and planets make up our **solar system.** The sun is a star like the stars you see in the sky at night. Some stars have solar systems with planets, too. There may be another planet out there that has an **atmosphere** with oxygen to breathe.

A star and the planets that orbit around it make up a solar system. Stars and solar systems make up a **galaxy.** Our galaxy is the Milky Way. It has about 100 billion stars. The Milky Way isn't the only galaxy. There are more galaxies in the **universe** than there are stars in a galaxy! How many? We don't know. There are too many, and many are too far away to see.

an orbit

a planet

A **comet** is a cloud of rock, ice, and gas that orbits the sun. Many earth years pass in its **journey** around the sun. Scientists keep **data** on comets to know when they will appear.

space

a comet

a galaxy

Think of the many galaxies in the universe. Think of the many stars in each galaxy. Think of the many planets that orbit the stars. Do you think that **extraterrestrials** may live on one of the planets? Many people **debate** this question.

3 **Discuss.** Work with a partner. What did you learn?

The sun is one of the 100 billion stars in our galaxy.

Our galaxy is called the Milky Way.

1 Listen, read, and sing. TR: 4.3

Deep in Outer Space

Let's all take a journey
past the atmosphere,
beyond our solar system,
far away from here.

We might find a new planet.
We might find a new place.
We might find things we've never seen
deep in outer space.

CHORUS

**Deep in outer space,
who knows what we might find?
Deep in outer space,
deep in outer space!**

Somewhere in the universe
we might find a moon
where flowers grow.
You never know,
but I wish we'd get there soon!

CHORUS

But right here on planet Earth
life is all around.
Our world is full of color,
texture, light, and sound.

We can take a journey
right outside our door
and see the wonder of life on Earth,
and so much more!

CHORUS

Deep in outer space.

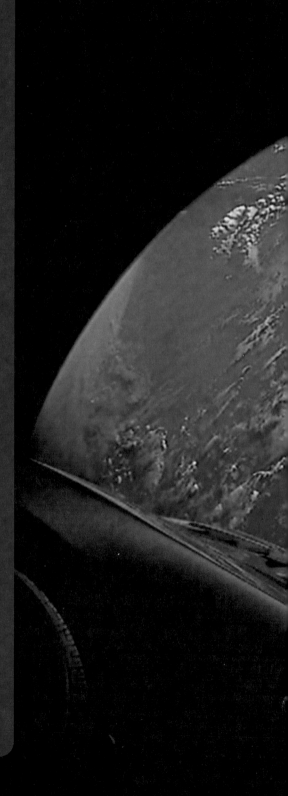

Roadster, launched by SpaceX,
heading toward Mars

Work with a partner. Take turns.

- moon
- planet
- solar system
- universe

GRAMMAR 1

> **May and might** TR: 4.4
>
> If a planet has an atmosphere, it **may** have life.
>
> There **might** be life on other planets.
>
> Do you think astronauts **might** go to the moon again?
>
> Yes, but it **may** be very simple life.

1 **Read.** Check the true sentences.

1. Some stars may have planets like Earth. ☐

2. We may find extraterrestrials on a distant planet. ☐

3. A meteor might hit Earth. ☐

4. The Milky Way might be a galaxy. ☐

5. Earth may have an atmosphere. ☐

6. You may become an astronaut. ☐

2 **Complete the sentences.**

> are   may be   is   may discover   live   may live

1. There _____ oxygen on planets in other galaxies.

2. There _____ no oxygen on the moon.

3. Extraterrestrials _____ on other planets.

4. Astronauts _____ on the space station for some time.

5. There _____ other solar systems in the universe.

6. One day, scientists _____ life on other planets.

3 **Write sentences.** What do you think?

1. green skin/extraterrestrial Extraterrestrials might not have green skin like they do in the movies.

2. comet/lifetime _____

_____

3. universe/galaxies _____

_____

4. comet/our planet _____

_____

5. find/life _____

_____

6. moon/one day _____

_____

4 **Talk about life in the universe.** Work in groups of three. Take turns to add more information.

There may be another planet with an atmosphere like Earth.

The planet might be too hot or too cold for life.

If the planet has water, it may have plants.

VOCABULARY 2

1 **Listen and repeat.**
Then read and write. TR: 4.5

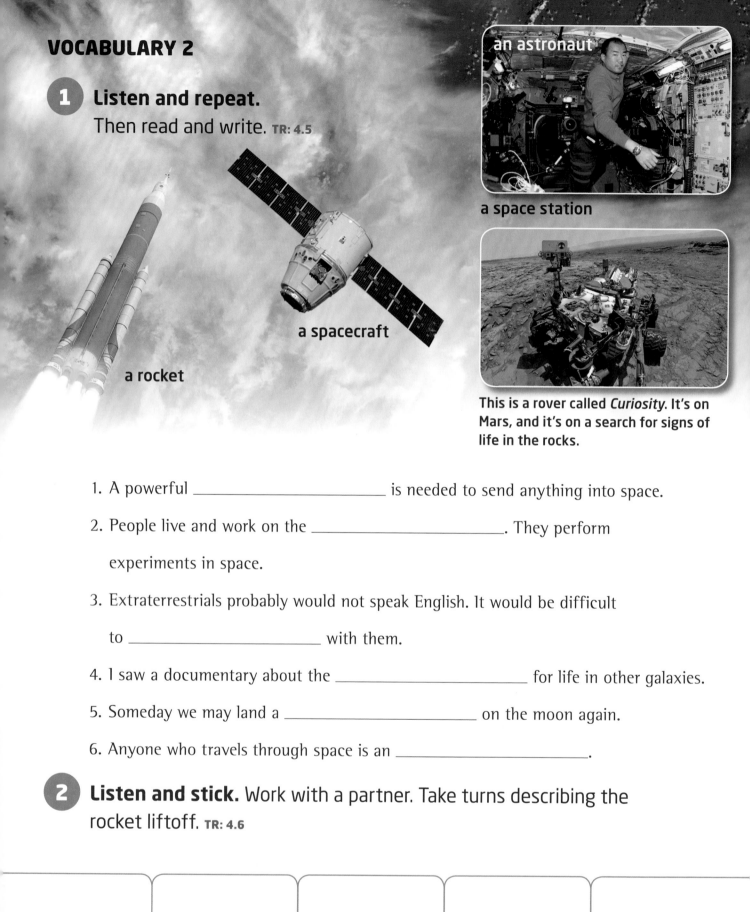

an astronaut

a space station

a spacecraft

a rocket

This is a rover called *Curiosity*. It's on Mars, and it's on a search for signs of life in the rocks.

1. A powerful _____ is needed to send anything into space.

2. People live and work on the _____. They perform experiments in space.

3. Extraterrestrials probably would not speak English. It would be difficult to _____ with them.

4. I saw a documentary about the _____ for life in other galaxies.

5. Someday we may land a _____ on the moon again.

6. Anyone who travels through space is an _____.

2 **Listen and stick.** Work with a partner. Take turns describing the rocket liftoff. TR: 4.6

| 1 | 2 | 3 | 4 | 5 |

GRAMMAR 2

Indefinite pronouns TR: 4.7

Did **everyone** see that comet?   Does **anyone** want to be an astronaut?
Someone will go to Mars one day.   **No one** can see all the stars in the universe.

1 **Read and write.** Complete the paragraph.

anyone   everyone   no one   someone

_____ likes to debate about life on other planets. _____

knows for sure if there is life on other planets or not. If _____ tells you

that they know, that person really doesn't know! Are you _____ who likes

to debate? I will debate about life in space with _____ who wants to.

_____ knows the answer, but _____ has an opinion!

2 **Ask and answer.** Work with a partner.

1. Does anyone in your family think there is life on other planets?
2. Name one thing everyone in your family does.
3. Name one thing no one in your family believes.
4. Name a funny habit someone in your family has.

3 **Play a game.** Cut out the cards in the back of the book. Make sentences.
Take turns.

69

1 Listen and read. TR: 4.8

Listening for Life

If extraterrestrials live on other planets, we can't see them. Planets in other solar systems are extremely far away. We can't see the planets, even with our biggest telescopes. But what if the extraterrestrials want to communicate with us? What if they are sending messages? This signal would travel through space. After many years, it might reach our solar system. It would be hidden in the noise from other places in space. We would need special tools to hear it.

Scientists at SETI (Search for Extraterrestrial Intelligence) have made a tool for listening. It uses 42 satellite dishes that are connected together. Scientists plan to have 350 dishes one day. They point all the dishes at the same place in the sky. Then they search for any data they can hear. The dishes can hear very weak signals. For example, they could hear a cell phone on a planet in our solar system. (That's if someone had a cell phone on Jupiter!) The dishes pick up noise from radios on Earth, too. Scientists must be careful to avoid this noise.

We have not heard from an extraterrestrial yet. But is it possible that they are listening to us? If they are, most could not have heard us yet. We have used radios for less than 100 years. That's not much time for the big distances in the universe. In that time, our signal could only reach a small number of stars. Extraterrestrials from nearby solar systems would not hear us for thousands of years.

Length of Time Needed for Radio Waves to Reach Earth

4.3 light years   431 light years   27,000 light years

2 Check T for *True* and F for *False*.

1. Extraterrestrials have listened to our radio waves for over 100 years. Ⓣ Ⓕ
2. SETI dishes listen for life by listening for radio signals. Ⓣ Ⓕ
3. Scientists point the SETI dishes in many directions. Ⓣ Ⓕ
4. Radio waves from Earth are a problem for SETI scientists. Ⓣ Ⓕ

3 Should we search for life? Write why and why not.

I think it's a good idea to search for life because . . .	I think it's a bad idea to search for life because . . .

4 Discuss the chart. Work with a partner. Support your opinions.

I think it's a good thing to search for life because we can learn many things from the extraterrestrials.

But how would we communicate with them?

 The first astronauts were fruit flies. They were launched on February 20, 1947.

2,480,000 light years

13,100,000,000 light years

The nearest

As far as we

WRITING

Persuasive Writing In persuasive writing, you write to convince the reader of your opinion. To persuade the reader, you use facts to support your opinion. Write strong sentences that show you believe in what you are saying. Introduce your facts with expressions such as *research shows, according to,* and *the facts show that.*

1 **Read.** How does the writer persuade? Underline the words.

Exploring Space

People spend a lot of time and money on space exploration. I think this is a good thing. We can learn a lot about our lives here on Earth when we discover more about space.

The facts show that many inventions we use today come from the technology people used to travel to space. For example, all smartphones today have a small camera. Space scientists started to make these in the 1990s so that they could take small cameras into space.

Also, according to experts, in many places the water we drink is now much cleaner because of space technology. Space scientists needed to search for ways to make water clean on the spacecraft. We use some of this technology today to keep our water clean on Earth.

I believe that searching for life in space is a good thing, too. It helps us to see how special our lives on Earth are.

2 **Write.** Do you think we should search for life in space? Take a position. Think about cost, usefulness, urgent problems on Earth, advances in technology, and so on. Use facts to persuade.

3 **Share.** Share your writing. Work in a small group. Listen and take notes.

Live curious.

Think. Pair. Share.

- How do you find answers to the things you want to know?

- Do you search for answers even when it's difficult?

- How do you feel when you finally find the answer?

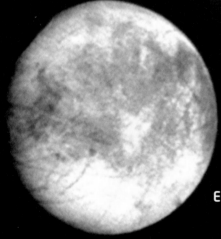

Europa

Jupiter

We finally have the tools and technology to answer this age-old question: Are we alone? Jupiter's moon Europa is a beautiful place to go and explore that question.**"**

Kevin Hand, Planetary Scientist/Astrobiologist, National Geographic Explorer

PROJECT

Make a model of a type of place where you think we could find life.

1. Use your imagination to re-create the surface of the type of planet or moon you choose. Use cardboard, paper, and other materials.

2. Make different life forms as you imagine them.

3. Think about how they might eat and what they might do.

4. Decide how to present your ideas to the class.

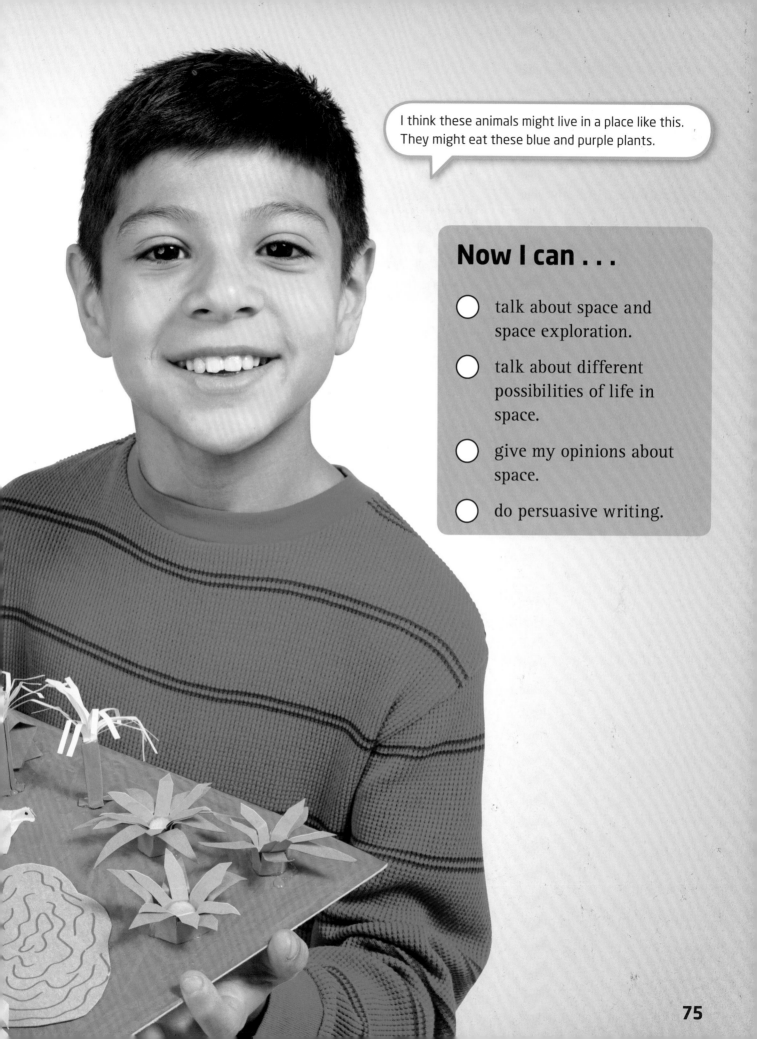

I think these animals might live in a place like this. They might eat these blue and purple plants.

Now I can . . .

○ talk about space and space exploration.

○ talk about different possibilities of life in space.

○ give my opinions about space.

○ do persuasive writing.

Arts Lost and Found

In this unit, I will . . .
- talk about traditions and communities.
- talk about different craft and cultural activities.
- understand changing traditions.
- write a blog entry.

Look and answer.

1. What is this person wearing?

   a. a hat   b. a mask

2. What is this person doing?

   a. dancing   b. singing

3. Use one word to describe the emotion on the face.

   _____

Traditional mask dancer, Colombo, Sri Lanka

VOCABULARY 1

1 **Listen and read.** TR: 5.1

2 **Listen and repeat.** TR: 5.2

Everyone should be **proud** of who they are. What makes you who you are? Part of who you are comes from the past. It comes from the **culture** of your parents, grandparents, and people before them. It comes from the **language** you speak, the **art** you see, the stories and music you hear, and the **traditions** you **share**.

Dragon boats are a 2,000-year-old Chinese tradition. Racers must cooperate and row together to win. Today dragon boat racing has become a modern world sport.

Storytelling isn't always done with words. In Laos, dancers tell stories with their hands. The dances are part of their history. This history is **passed down** from one **generation** to the next.

The people of Tabasco, Mexico, keep their history alive. This **local** boy has clay on his face. He will do the jaguar dance to bring rain. His people speak an old language that came from the Olmec thousands of years ago.

The people of Ghana **hold on** to their tradition of **weaving** beautiful cloth. **Tourists** come to Ghana to buy cloth. The money that the tourists pay helps the **future** of the **community**.

3 **Discuss.**
What did you learn?

In Laos, they use their hands as part of their dance.

Their hands tell stories.

1 **Listen, read, and sing.** TR: 5.3

Keep Your Culture Strong

CHORUS

**Knowing your history is important.
Holding on to your culture is an
excellent thing!
Knowing your history is important.
It's up to you to keep your culture strong!**

What special art does your culture bring to
our world?
What special thing does your family bring to
our world?
Weaving? Learn to do it!
Storytelling? Learn to tell it!
What brings your culture pride?

CHORUS

What special art does your culture bring to
our world?
What special thing does your family bring to
our world?
Embroidery? Learn to sew it!
Sculpture? Learn to sculpt it!
What brings your culture pride?

Your grandparents may seem old to you,
but they know a thing or two!

CHORUS

2 **Ask and answer.** Work with a partner.

1. What special art does your culture bring
   to our world?
2. What special thing does your family bring
   to our world?
3. What would you like to learn to do?

Ceremonial dancers,
California, USA

GRAMMAR 1

Gerunds as subjects TR: 5.4

Knowing your history is important.
Holding on to your traditions is a good thing.
Passing down family stories connects generations.
Creating art is a good way to share your culture.

1 **Read.** Complete the sentences.

cook   make   paint   row   share   weave

1. _____ a boat is hard to do with another person.

2. _____ cloth was my grandmother's work.

3. _____ art is exciting!

4. _____ your traditions helps other people

understand you.

5. _____ on wood is fun for people who like colors.

6. _____ traditional recipes is another way to keep

your culture alive.

2 **Write.** Complete the sentences about you and your family.

1. Painting *is my father's hobby.* _____.

2. Teaching _____.

3. Cooking _____.

4. Helping _____.

5. Taking photos _____.

6. Reading _____.

3 Complete the conversation.

Mario: Grandpa, did you **listen to music** when you were a kid?

Grandpa: Yes, I did. _____ was one of my favorite hobbies!

Mario: And did you **go to the movies?**

Grandpa: Of course! I went every Sunday. _____ was the most important event of the weekend!

Mario: Did you **talk** to your friends **on the phone?**

Grandpa: No, I didn't. _____ was very expensive when I was a kid!

Mario: And did you **play sports?**

Grandpa: Not much. My parents thought that _____ was a waste of time. They wanted me to study all the time! But I still played soccer with my friends!

Mario: How about chores? Did you **help around the house?**

Grandpa: Of course! _____ was something everyone had to do!

4 Give your opinion. Work in groups of three. Take turns.

| listening to stories | making art | saving traditions | visiting family |
| watching dancers | singing traditional songs | looking at old photos |

Looking at my grandfather's old photos is really cool!

VOCABULARY 2

1 **Listen and repeat.** Then read and write. TR: 5.5

sculpture

embroidery

handcrafted

pottery

jewelry making

1. When a work of art is made by hand, we say it's _____.

2. People use _____ to make their clothes more beautiful and decorative.

3. _____ is made from clay that dries and becomes hard. Sometimes it is heated in an oven.

4. To make a _____, artists can use materials such as wood, stone, metal, or ice.

5. _____ is popular. Many kids like to make bracelets.

2 **Look, rank (1 = most favorite), and stick.** Work with a partner. Discuss your preferences.

1	2	3	4	5

GRAMMAR 2

Gerunds as objects TR: 5.6

My friends are good at **making** jewelry.
I like **eating** traditional foods.
My mother enjoys **embroidering** clothes.
I'm interested in **learning** about new places.

1 **Read and complete the sentences.** Use the words from the list.

cooperating   making   passing   sharing   storytelling   traveling

1. Young people today are very interested in _____ their

   traditions.

2. I'm very excited about _____ where my grandparents

   came from.

3. Do you like _____? Storytellers like

   _____ down their traditions.

4. I enjoy _____ traditional jewelry.

2 **Play a game.** Cut out the cube in the back of the book. Work with a partner. Take turns making sentences.

Playing. I enjoy playing soccer with my friends.

Great! My turn.

1 **Listen and read.** TR: 5.7

Not Your Grandpa's Mariachi

There's a new band in town. They're playing a traditional style of Mexican music called *mariachi* . . . but with a twist. Before meeting this new band, let's step back in time.

Mariachi music started hundreds of years ago, but the traditional style we see today began in the 19th century. Groups of farmers played together. Their instruments included traditional violins and different kinds of classical guitars. The smaller guitars played the higher notes, and a traditional bass guitar played the low ones. They had trumpets, too. The music was often loud, happy, and exciting, but it could also be quiet and romantic. The musicians wore traditional suits with silver buttons and a sombrero, a wide Mexican hat.

The mariachi played and danced at celebrations such as birthdays and weddings. As people from Mexico moved around the world, the mariachi tradition spread, too. In the past, mariachi bands were always men and they always sang in Spanish.

Fast forward to today and meet the Mariachi Flor de Toloache. They're an all-women mariachi band. The band met in New York, in the USA. Some of the women have Mexican or Puerto Rican families, but others do not. So the band sometimes sings in Spanish and sometimes in English. They sing traditional songs, but they also sing versions of modern songs in a mariachi style. They still dress in traditional mariachi suits. The band is building on the mariachi tradition and making mariachi music to fit today's modern world.

Flor de Toloache,
Mariachi Band,
Brooklyn, New York, USA

2 Read and write.

1. Where did mariachi music begin? _____

2. What instruments are usually in a mariachi band? _____

3. When did the traditional mariachi that we see today begin? _____

4. What language do mariachi singers usually sing in? _____

5. Where did the Mariachi Flor de Toloache band meet? _____

3 Write. Compare traditional mariachi to the Mariachi Flor de Toloache.

	traditional mariachi	Mariachi Flor de Toloache
male or female		
choice of songs		
dress		
language		

4 Make new music. Work with a partner. Invent a new musical style. It can be completely new, or you can modernize a style you know. What styles would you mix? What instruments would you use?

Let's mix tango and rock!

Yes! Let's add drums and an electric guitar! Any other ideas?

weird but true

Mice sing to each other at night.

87

WRITING

Blog Entry In a personal blog, you write about your thoughts. You describe what you saw, heard, or felt. A blog sounds like an informal conversation. You can imagine you are talking to your friends and use informal expressions like *awesome* and *cool*. You can ask your readers to post a response on your blog, too.

1 **Read.** What informal expressions does the writer use in her blog? Underline them.

« » ➕ 🔊 Cecilia's Blog

The coolest vacation ever!!!

My family and I went to Machu Picchu in Peru. It was awesome. First, I took a long train ride with my family to Aguas Calientes. From there we took a bus to Machu Picchu. The bus went slowly up the steep mountain. (I'm really glad the bus was slow.) LOL. From the bus window, I saw llamas eating grass.

When we arrived, I was excited. It was so cool to see the ruins. The Incas who built Machu Picchu were great architects. My family and I climbed the stairs all the way up to the Sun Gate. It was a difficult climb. We stopped to rest a few times because I was incredibly tired. Then we were at the top—what a view! We could see everything! I think my photos are fabulous. Tell me what you think.

2 **Write.** Write a blog entry about a family vacation or a special day. Describe your thoughts and feelings.

3 **Share.** Share your writing. Work in a small group. Listen and take notes.

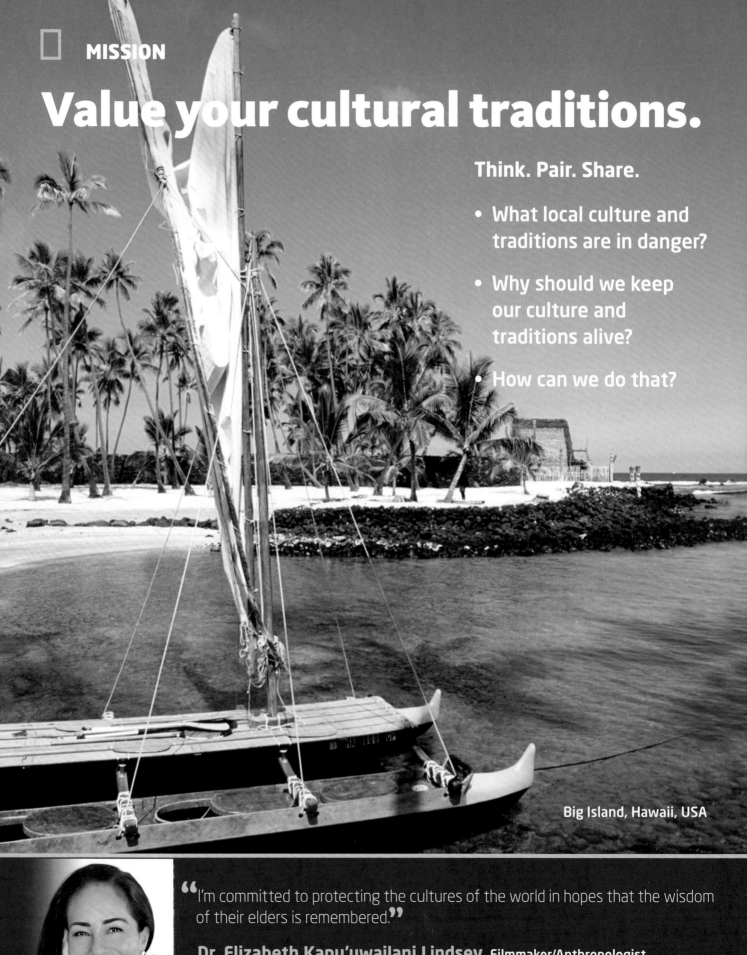

MISSION

Value your cultural traditions.

Think. Pair. Share.

- What local culture and traditions are in danger?

- Why should we keep our culture and traditions alive?

- How can we do that?

Big Island, Hawaii, USA

"I'm committed to protecting the cultures of the world in hopes that the wisdom of their elders is remembered."

Dr. Elizabeth Kapu'uwailani Lindsey, Filmmaker/Anthropologist,
National Geographic Explorer

PROJECT

Make a museum of the future.

1 Find an object that is important to you that you think people in the future would find interesting.

2 Write about why it is important to you.

3 Put all the objects together in part of your classroom.

4 Invite people to come to your museum of the future.

I love this lantern. It's made of silk and it has been in my family for a long time. We often hang it up outside our home in the evening. I love looking at it when it's shining!

Now I can . . .

- ◯ talk about traditions and communities.
- ◯ talk about different craft and cultural activities.
- ◯ understand changing traditions.
- ◯ write a blog entry.

Unit 6

Amazing Plants!

In this unit, I will . . .
- describe plants.
- talk about what plants and animals do to help plants survive.
- compare how plants grow and adapt.
- do descriptive writing.

Check T for *True* and F for *False*.

1. These flowers are sculptures. (T) (F)

2. The flowers are wet. (T) (F)

3. These flowers eat insects. (T) (F)

Australian sundew

VOCABULARY 1

1 Listen and read. TR: 6.1

2 Listen and repeat. TR: 6.2

Have you ever heard of a flower that smells like rotting meat to **attract** insects? Have you seen a plant close its **leaves** over an insect? Can plants really do these things? Let's learn more about the **behavior** of plants.

Pitcher plant

Plants need **light,** air, water, and nutrients to live. **Roots** absorb the nutrients that are in the **ground** and water. Tiny creatures called **bacteria** turn these nutrients into food that the plant can use. But some places don't have a lot of these nutrients. So some plants **adapt**. They follow a different plan for **survival**. Their **strategy** is to eat insects to live!

Stink lily, Panama

Venus flytrap, Southern Brazil

a leaf

a stem

The stink lily gets its name from its smell. The flower **stinks** like rotting meat. The smell attracts flies to the plant—and then **tricks** them! When a fly crawls on the flower, pollen sticks to the fly. Then the fly takes the pollen and leaves it on the next plant it visits. That's how the stink lily makes new plants.

The Venus flytrap attracts insects with a sweet odor. When an insect lands on an open leaf, the leaf closes and **traps** the insect. Then the plant slowly **digests** the insect over a period of eight to ten days.

3 **Ask and answer.** Work with a partner. What did you learn?

How do plants adapt to survive?

Some plants trap insects.

95

1 **Listen, read, and sing.** TR: 6.3

Plants Are All Around

CHORUS

**Leaf and stem and flower and root!
The sweet, delicious smell of fruit
is here and there and everywhere!
Plants are all around.**

**Plants are growing
up and down.
Air is flowing
all around.**

Plants come in every shape and size.
Their bright colors attract the eyes
of bees and butterflies.

Big and small,
plants survive it all.

CHORUS

Some plants play tricks with our eyes.
They're made to give us a surprise.
A plant is designed to survive.
To make new seeds, to grow and thrive.

Some of the oldest plants on Earth
are trees on mountains high,
drinking in the light,
reaching up into the sky.

Leaf and stem and flower and root!
The sweet, delicious smell of fruit
is here and there and everywhere!
Plants are all around.

2 **Ask and answer.** Work with a partner.

1. Which plants do you like best?
2. Do you eat them?
3. What makes them special to you?

A monkey orchid

GRAMMAR 1

The passive: Simple present TR: 6.4

Insects **are attracted** to the plant's sweet smell.
The seeds **are carried** away by birds.

How **is** the insect **trapped?**
The fly **is caught** inside the closing leaf.

1 **Read.** Complete the sentences.

1. Plant food (make) _____is made_____ by bacteria.

2. Pollen (take) _____ to other plants by insects.

3. The seeds (carry) _____ by birds.

4. Plants that eat insects (find) _____ in the rain forest.

5. Many new plants (discover) _____ every year.

2 **Read.** Underline the answer.

Socotra **is located / is called** in the Indian Ocean. Many strange trees
are found / are needed here. One famous tree **is attracted / is called** the
dragon blood tree. It **is used / is found** to make paint and medicine.

The desert rose **is used / is found** in the desert in Socotra. It has beautiful
pink flowers. It **is shaped / is found** like the foot of an elephant!

Dragon blood trees

3 **Read and write.** Rewrite the sentences.

1. Plants need nutrients for survival.

   Nutrients are needed by plants for survival.

2. Birds eat the fruit.

   _____

3. The plant attracts insects.

   _____

4. The smell of the stink lily tricks the flies.

   _____

5. The pitcher plant traps and digests small animals.

   _____

4 **Make sentences.** Work with a partner. Take turns. How many can you make?

snacks	need	children
flowers	find	plants
insects	eat	flowers

Flowers are eaten by plants.

That's not true!

VOCABULARY 2

1 **Listen and repeat.** Then read and write. TR: 6.5

a petal

a daisy

a vine

a thorn

a rose

1. An outer part of a flower is called a _____.

2. A climbing _____ holds onto things as it grows.

3. Be careful! That _____ is sharp.

4. The class gave the teacher a red _____.

5. Is that flower a white _____?

2 **Guess and stick.** Work with a partner. Give a clue. Take turns.

> That's a pretty yellow flower!

> It's a daisy!

1   2   3   4   5

GRAMMAR 2

Relative clauses with *that* TR: 6.6

I don't want a plant **that** smells like rotting meat!
I like plants **that** trick and trap insects.

1 **Read and write.**

> sunflower/stem   daisy/petals   garden/flowers   rain forest/vines
> rose/thorns   tree/leaves   Venus flytrap/insects

1. A sunflower is a plant that has a long stem.

2. _____

3. _____

4. _____

5. _____

6. _____

7. _____

2 **Play a game.** Work in groups of three. Choose a page in this book. Describe an object. The group guesses what it is. The winner picks another page.

Go to page 63. This is something that flies through space.

It's a rocket.

No. Guess again.

It's a comet!

1 **Listen and read.** TR: 6.7

Is *That* a **Plant?**

The *Hydnora africana* has no leaves or stem. It has a flower that looks like a hungry mouth! Inside is white stuff that stinks. Insects are attracted to the smell. The insect is trapped inside the flower by stiff hairs. The insect eats the white stuff to survive. Pollen sticks to the insect. A few days later, the flower opens, and the insect is free. Then it takes the pollen to another flower. The flower has done its job!

The white baneberry is also called "doll's eyes." Its fruit looks like eyes on blood-red stems! It is round and white and has a black dot. Birds eat the fruit and spread the seeds. That's how the doll's eyes makes other plants. The fruit does not hurt the birds, but it's poisonous to people! If people touch any part of the plant, they will get blisters! Eating the fruit can stop a person's heart.

The *Rafflesia arnoldii* also has no leaves or stem. But it has the largest flower of all plants! It can grow to be 1 meter (3 feet) across and can weigh 11 kilos (24 pounds). The flower looks scary. Things that look like big thorns grow out of its center. And worse, it stinks like rotting meat—just like the stink lily! But this plant doesn't eat insects. The odor attracts insects that carry its pollen to other plants. This big flower blooms for only five days. Because there are fewer and fewer of these plants, they may become extinct.

Mt. Kinabalu, Borneo

2 Check T for *True* and F for *False*.

1. The white baneberry has a stinky smell that attracts insects.　(T)　(F)

2. The fruit of the *Hydnora africana* is very poisonous.　(T)　(F)

3. The *Rafflesia arnoldii* has no leaves or stems.　(T)　(F)

4. Birds avoid the white baneberry.　(T)　(F)

5. The *Rafflesia arnoldii* eats insects that walk on it.　(T)　(F)

6. When the *Hydnora africana* traps an insect, it lets it go in a few days.　(T)　(F)

3 Rank the plants. Work with a partner (1 = most favorite). Explain why.

Rank	Plant	Why the plant is cool
	Hydnora africana	
	Rafflesia arnoldii	
	Rose	
	Venus flytrap	
	White baneberry	
	Your choice _____	

4 Invent a cool plant. Work in a small group. Draw the plant and say what it does. Share your ideas.

	Leaves & stems	Poisonous	Stinky	Flower size	Fruit
Hydnora africana			✔	6 cm (2.36 in.)	✔
Rafflesia arnoldii			✔	1 m (3.28 ft.)	✔
White baneberry	✔	✔		10 cm (3.93 in.)	✔

WRITING

Descriptive Writing In descriptive writing, you describe what something looks like and what it does. You can describe the big parts first and then the small parts. Or you can go from top to bottom, or one end to the other. Then you can describe how it works.

1 **Read.** Read about the sensitive plant. How does the writer describe it? How does the writer organize the description?

The Sensitive Plant

Did you know that some plants can move? The sensitive plant moves when you touch it. The stem has tiny white hairs, and it stands straight up. It grows to about 50 centimeters. It has many thin green leaves. Each thin leaf is made of many tiny parts. The parts are like tiny leaves. These tiny leaves grow on both sides of each leaf stem.

When you touch a leaf, the tiny leaves fold. Two by two, starting from where you touch, they close down. The leaf stem hangs down, too. It looks like it is hiding and doesn't want you to touch it. After a half hour, the plant stands up—until you touch it again!

Sensitive plant

2 **Write.** Write about the plant you invented on the previous page. Describe it. What does it look like? What does it do? Organize your description.

3 **Share.** Share your writing. Work in a small group. Listen and take notes.

Value plants.

Think. Pair. Share.

- What plants are important in your community?

- Why are these plants important?

- How are they used?

Ecofriendly hotel, Singapore

"On my first trip to the rain forest I met a woman who was in terrible pain because no one in her village could remember which plant would cure her. I saw that knowledge was truly being lost, and in that moment I knew this was what I wanted to do with my life."

Maria Fadiman Ethnobotanist, National Geographic Explorer

PROJECT

Make a local plant guide.

1 Work with a partner. Choose a local plant.

2 Research the plant. Collect or draw pictures.

3 Glue and label the pictures.

4 Describe the plant and how it is used.

The aloe vera plant has thick pointy leaves. It is used for sunburns.

Aloe Vera Plant

Aloe vera comes from Africa, but it grows in many places. It doesn't have a stem. It has very thick pointy leaves. It likes full sun. It is good for sunburns.

Now I can . . .

○ describe plants.

○ talk about what plants and animals do to help plants survive.

○ compare how plants grow and adapt.

○ do descriptive writing.

Review

1 **Read.** Complete the paragraphs. Use words from the list.

adapt	embroidery	handcrafted	no one	tourists
anyone	extraterrestrial	hold on	strategy	trap
astronaut	galaxy	leaves	survival	weave

1. Do you think _____ is listening to us from outer

   space? _____ knows the answer to this

   question, but scientists are discussing the possibility of

   intelligent _____ life.

2. The Huichol people in Mexico make traditional art to help them

   _____ to their culture. Selling their _____ art

   to _____ helps the future of their community.

3. The resurrection fern has learned to _____ to dry climates. When

   there isn't enough rain, it looks dead. But this is just a _____

   for _____. The plant is alive! When it rains, the dry

   _____ turn green.

2 **Role-play.** Work with a partner. Practice and perform for the class.

> **Student A:**
>   You think there may be
>   life on other planets.

> **Student B:**
>   You don't believe there is
>   life on other planets.

anyone	everyone	journey	no one	someone	universe
communicate	galaxy	may/might	planet	spacecraft	

> I think there may be life on planets
> in other solar systems.

> If you're right, why doesn't anyone from
> other planets communicate with us?

3 **Listen.** Work with a partner. Listen to the sentences. Then read the sentences below. Check T for *True* and F for *False*. TR: 6.8

1. Traditions are passed down from one generation to the next. (T) (F)

2. Languages must be protected from dying. (T) (F)

3. Some plants are trapped by flies. (T) (F)

4. Insect-eating plants are called *carnivorous*. (T) (F)

5. The possibility of human life has been debated by extraterrestrials for a long time. (T) (F)

4 **Work in small groups.**

1. Write eight definitions using the word *that* on strips of paper.
2. Cut the strips just before the word *that*.
3. Mix up the paper strips, and exchange your paper strips with another group.
4. Match the strips of paper, and read the sentences aloud. The group with the most correct sentences wins.

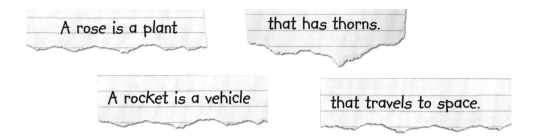

A rose is a plant   that has thorns.

A rocket is a vehicle   that travels to space.

5 **Write.** Choose four objects from the list. Write clues for your partner to guess.

comet	rocket	space station
jewelry	satellite	TV
pottery	sculpture	vine

This is something that is pretty and often made of gold. People wear it on their fingers or around their necks.

Jewelry!

1 Listen and read. TR: 6.9

Attack of the *Extraterrestrial* Plants!

SCENE 1
FADE IN: SPACE-LIKE MUSIC
FADE TO: INTERIOR OF SPACECRAFT
CONTROL ROOM—DAY

MAYA looks at a strange plant in the corner of the control room while JAKE works on his tablet.

MAYA: Have you seen this?

JAKE: What is it?

MAYA: I don't know. It's growing out of the corner. It's blue.

JAKE: (ignoring her) That's interesting, but I'm busy.

MAYA: It has leaves and a stem . . .

JAKE: If I don't finish with this data, the captain will be angry—

MAYA: (puzzled) It might be a plant, but how can anything grow here?

Suddenly, a high-pitched sound comes from the plant.

JAKE: Is that some new music that you're listening to?

MAYA: (irritated) No. It's the plant. It might be trying to communicate with us.

JAKE: (now paying attention) In plant language? Oh . . . . It's turning orange. It might be upset?

MAYA: (examining it more closely) The roots might be coming from the space sample room. Let's look.

FADE OUT: JAKE AND MAYA EXIT
FADE IN: SOFT STRANGE PLANT-LIKE SOUNDS THEN AUTOMATIC DOOR OPENING

Maya and Jake walk into a room. It's full of strange moving plants—most of them are blue. They are all making loud humming noises.

MAYA: (surprised and worried) Look at the plants! Who put them here?

JAKE: (examining a plant closely and pulling off a leaf) They may be more intelligent than they look. I'll just pull off this leaf—

The room explodes in angry plant noises and the plants turn purple and start to move toward Jake.

MAYA: Oh no! They're turning purple.

JAKE: (still examining the plants) Are they plants . . . . or are they extraterrestrials?

The plants move toward Jake.

MAYA: (shouting at Jake as the plants start to attack him) Watch out! They're coming for you! Run!

FADE OUT: AGGRESSIVE PLANT SOUNDS PLUS SPACE-LIKE MUSIC

2 **Match to complete the sentences.**

1. Jake   turn purple when they are angry.

2. Maya   doesn't listen to Maya.

3. The plants in the sample room   is working on some data.

4. At first, Jake   finds a strange blue plant.

3 **Read.** Work with a partner to write stage directions.

1. MAYA: "I don't know. It's growing out of the corner. It's blue."

Maya is scared and shaking as she points to the plant
and slowly walks toward it.

2. JAKE: "That's interesting, but I'm busy."

_____

_____

3. JAKE: "Is that some new music that you're listening to?"

_____

_____

4. MAYA: "Oh no! They're turning purple!"

_____

_____

5. MAYA: "Watch out! They're coming for you!"

_____

_____

4 **Express yourself.** Choose an activity.

1. What happens next? Write the next scene.

2. Act out your own space invasion. Write the scene and perform it.

3. In a group, act out scene 1. You'll need a director, two actors, and a plant.

Let's Talk

Can I borrow your bike?

I will . . .
- make an informal request.
- make an excuse.
- show understanding / accept "no" for an answer.

1 **Listen and read.** TR: 6.10

Lucia: Hey, **can I borrow** your bike this weekend, Roberto?

Roberto: Um, **I'm really sorry,** but it's new. My dad won't let me lend it.

Lucia: **That's OK. I understand.** Marcelo, **can you lend me** *your* bike?

Marcelo: **Sure. Go ahead.** But give it back on Sunday, OK?

Lucia: **Thanks a lot.**

Can I borrow . . . ? Can you lend me . . . ? Is it OK if I use . . . ?	I'm really sorry. I'm sorry, but . . . I can't. It isn't mine.	That's OK. I understand. No problem. Don't worry.
	Sure. Go ahead. Sure. Here you are! Yeah, you can borrow _____ . Sure. I can lend you _____ . Of course.	Thanks a lot. Thanks. I'll give it back later.

2 **Discuss.** Work with a partner. Use the chart. Take turns to lend and borrow objects.

It could work.

I will . . .
- make a suggestion.
- agree and disagree.
- counter.

3 **Listen and read.** TR: 6.11

Lin: **I think we should** interview a scientist for our project.
Cheng: **That's a great idea.**
Mei: **Yeah, but** we don't have the time.
Jiang: **Actually, that could work.** My uncle is a scientist! I'll text him!

I think we should _____ .	**That's a great idea.**	**Yeah, but** _____ .	**Actually, that could work.**
I know what we should do! We should . . . Why don't we . . . ? What if we . . . ?	Why not? That could be good.	I don't think that'll work. I'm not so sure.	That might work. In fact, I think _____ . We could also _____ .

4 **Listen.** You will hear two discussions. Does everyone agree at the end of the discussion? Circle the answer. TR: 6.12

1. Yes   No
2. Yes   No

5 **Discuss.** Work in a group. Prepare and practice discussions. Choose one of the three situations given below.

1. Let's interview a famous person!
2. Why don't we do a report with a big map?
3. I think we should paint a mural of volcanoes on the classroom wall.

Volcanoes

In this unit, I will . . .
- discuss volcanoes.
- describe how a volcano erupts.
- make predictions.
- write a process description.

Check T for *True* and F for *False*.

1. Red-hot rocks are thrown into the air. Ⓣ Ⓕ

2. The lava flows down the volcano. Ⓣ Ⓕ

3. The lava shines in the dark. Ⓣ Ⓕ

4. Do you want to visit this place? Explain.

Stromboli Volcano, Sicily, Italy

VOCABULARY 1

1 Listen and read. TR: 7.1

2 Listen and repeat. TR: 7.2

Go for a walk on a sunny day. The earth seems **calm** under your feet. But **deep** down, it is not. Under the earth's crust, it is so hot that rock is **melted**. This melted rock is called *magma*.

In some places, there are deep **cracks** in the **surface** of the earth. These cracks let magma come to the surface. The magma pushes up the earth's crust. It **creates** a mountain—a **volcano!**

A volcano **erupts** when magma **explodes** onto the surface. The flow of melted rock is called *lava*. The lava is thrown into the air and flows down the volcano. The **heat** of the lava burns everything it touches.

The blast of an eruption throws **steam** into the air. The steam is created from water **inside** the earth. The blast also sends **gases** high into the sky. They make breathing difficult. A volcanic eruption can fill the sky with **ash**. The ash can come down and **cover** the land with a **thick** layer.

surface   inside

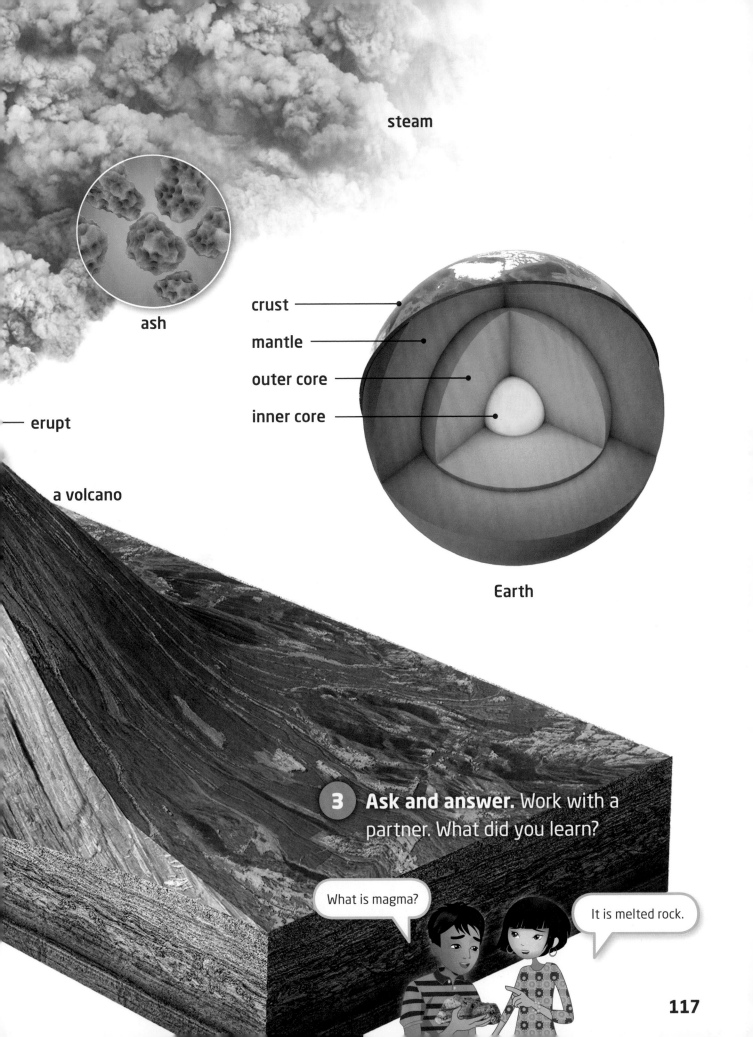

steam

ash

crust

mantle

outer core

inner core

erupt

a volcano

Earth

3 **Ask and answer.** Work with a partner. What did you learn?

What is magma?

It is melted rock.

117

1 **Listen, read, and sing.** TR: 7.3

Volcanoes Are a Lot Like Me

CHORUS
Volcanoes are a lot like me.
Some are awake and full of energy.
Other volcanoes are sleeping.
Yes, volcanoes are a lot like me!

When I get really silly,
and my energy builds up,
if it has no place to go,
sometimes I think I will explode!

Deep inside a volcano,
heat and gas are building up.
If they have no place to go,
the volcano will erupt!

CHORUS

If a volcano is dormant,
it's really just asleep.
A dormant volcano will sleep for centuries.

If a volcano is active,
it's very wide awake.
When it's awake, it's just like me.
It's ready to blow off some energy!

CHORUS

2 **Discuss.** Work with a partner.

1. Sometimes I'm like an active
   volcano because . . .
2. Sometimes I'm like a dormant
   volcano because . . .

Volcanic eruption in the
Eyjafjallajokull Glacier, Iceland

GRAMMAR 1

First conditional TR: 7.4

If the lava **touches** the trees, it **will** burn them.
If rain **hits** the lava, it**'ll** turn to steam.
I **will go** to a safe place **if** the volcano **erupts**.
The plants **will burn if** hot ash **covers** them.

1 **Read.** Write sentences.

1. I go to Hawaii / I see volcanoes

_____

2. I run away / volcano erupts

_____

3. ash covers the grass / the grass dies

_____

4. lava reaches the sea / it makes steam

_____

5. no airplanes fly / ash fills the sky

_____

Kīlauea, Hawaii, USA

2 **Write.** Write five sentence halves beginning with *if.* Work in pairs. Take turns. Complete each other's sentences.

1. If *I go to a volcano to take pictures*_____,
   *I will be very careful*_____.

2. If _____,
   _____.

3. If _____,
   _____.

4. If _____,
   _____.

5. If _____,
   _____.

6. If _____,
   _____.

3 **Make sentences.** Work in small groups. Build each new sentence on the one before.

If it rains, I will get wet.

If I get wet, I'll catch a cold.

VOCABULARY 2

1 **Listen and repeat.** Then read and write. TR: 7.5

dormant

cone
active

crater
extinct

1. If a volcano is erupting, then it is _____.

2. If a volcano is not erupting, but may erupt in the future, it is

   _____.

3. If a volcano has not erupted in thousands of years and will

   not erupt in the future, it is _____.

4. The hole left at the top of a volcano that has erupted is called a

   _____.

5. The sides of a volcano form the _____ at the top.

2 **Listen and stick in order.** Work with a partner. Discuss. TR: 7.6

How does he know the volcano is extinct?

He read about it before climbing.

1   2   3   4   5

GRAMMAR 2

Because of . . . TR: 7.7

Because of the ash, the animals could not breathe.
The trees died **because of** the heat from the lava.

1 **Read and write.**

1. rocks flew into the sky / the eruption

_____

2. the heat / no one could get close to the crater

_____

3. it was difficult to see / the ash

_____

4. we saw white clouds in the sky / the steam

_____

5. the blast / the eruption could be heard from far away

_____

2 **Play a game.** Play with a partner. Cut out the cards in the back of the book and put them face down in a pile. Choose a card and start a sentence. Complete your partner's sentences.

Because of the ash …

we couldn't play outside.

1 **Listen and read.** TR: 7.8

The largest known volcano is on Mars. It is about 22,000 m tall and 700 km across!

ACTIVE Volcanoes

There are active volcanoes all over the world. Some erupt often, sending hot lava down their slopes. People often live near these volcanoes. Because of the ash, the land is good for farming.

The longest-erupting volcano is Mount Etna, in Sicily. It has been active for 3,500 years. Mount Etna erupts very often. It has destroyed many towns. People have tried to change the lava flow. They've built earth walls and used explosives. Some towns have avoided destruction. Successful evacuation plans have kept people safe.

Five volcanoes created the island of Hawaii. Mauna Loa is the largest volcano in the world. Kīlauea is one of the most active. In fact, it almost never stops erupting. In 2018, lava flowed through the streets of some towns near the volcano. Many people lost their homes.

The volcano Nyamuragira, in Africa, erupts about every two years. It also has big lava flows. It creates smaller volcanoes on its sides. At one time, the volcano had a crater with a lake of lava. Then in 1938, there was an eruption that opened up one side of the volcano. Because of the eruption, the lava lake flowed out of the crater. People do not live near this volcano.

Fuego is an active volcano in Guatemala. There was a sudden and powerful eruption in June of 2018. Many nearby towns were covered in ash. The international airport in Guatemala City had to close because there was too much ash on the runway.

Kīlauea, Hawaii, USA

2 **Read and circle the letter.**

1. This volcano had a lake of lava.

   a. Mount Etna   b. Nyamuragira   c. Fuego

2. This is the largest volcano in the Hawaiian Islands.

   a. Mauna Loa   b. Kīlauea   c. Fuego

3. This volcano's eruption caused an airport to close.

   a. Nyamuragira   b. Fuego   c. Kīlauea

4. This volcano is the longest-erupting volcano.

   a. Kīlauea   b. Nyamuragira   c. Mount Etna

3 **Where are these volcanoes?** Work with a partner.

Kīlauea
Mount Etna
Nyamuragira
Mauna Loa
Fuego

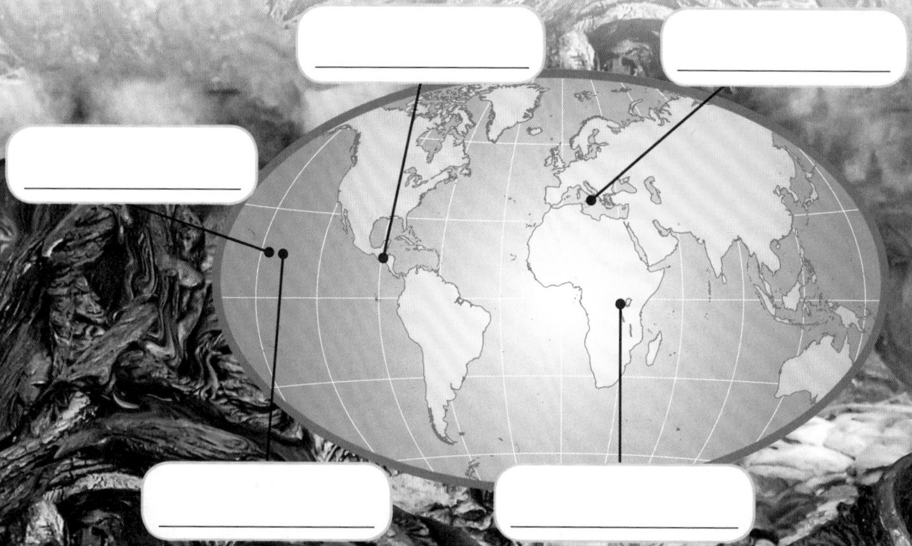

4 **Work with a partner.** Read the text again. Talk about two volcanoes. Take turns. Take notes.

	Name of Volcano	Notes
1		
2		

WRITING

Process Description A process description explains what happens in a sequence. It follows a series of actions from beginning to end. Use words such as *first, then, next, after, when, while, at the same time, now, before, as long as,* and *finally.* These words show the order in which actions or stages happen.

1 **Read.** Read the paragraphs about the stages of a volcanic eruption. How does the writer show the sequence of events? Underline the words.

How a Volcano Erupts

A volcanic eruption is a process that starts inside the earth.

The big hole under the volcano is called the *magma chamber.* First, the chamber starts to fill with hot magma. At the same time, hot gas fills the chamber. When the chamber is full of gas and magma, it has to escape through the top of the volcano. So the gas and magma start to go up the cone of the volcano.

Then the volcano erupts. It throws ash high into the air. At the same time, lava flows down the sides. The volcano erupts for as long as the magma and gas push up. This can last a long time.

Finally, the volcano calms down and it stops erupting. But the process could start again at any moment!

2 **Write.** Describe a process that you know. Explain the steps from beginning to end.

3 **Share.** Share your writing. Work in a small group. Listen and take notes.

Help in a disaster.

Think. Pair. Share.

- What types of disasters happen around the world?

- What can you do to help in a disaster?

- How can you get your community to help?

Eldfell Volcano, Iceland

"Crisis mapping can pinpoint urgent needs instantly, saving time and lives."

Patrick Meier, Crisis Mapper, National Geographic Explorer

PROJECT

Make a model of an erupting volcano.

1. Get a cardboard tube about 4 cm wide and 20 cm long.

2. Cover the bottom of the tube with clay. Stick the tube up on cardboard.

3. Crush balls of newspaper. Tape them to the tube to make a cone.

4. Cover the cone with aluminum foil. Paint it or glue sand on it.

5. Fill half the tube with baking soda.

6. Add red food color to vinegar. Pour it in the tube, and watch it erupt!

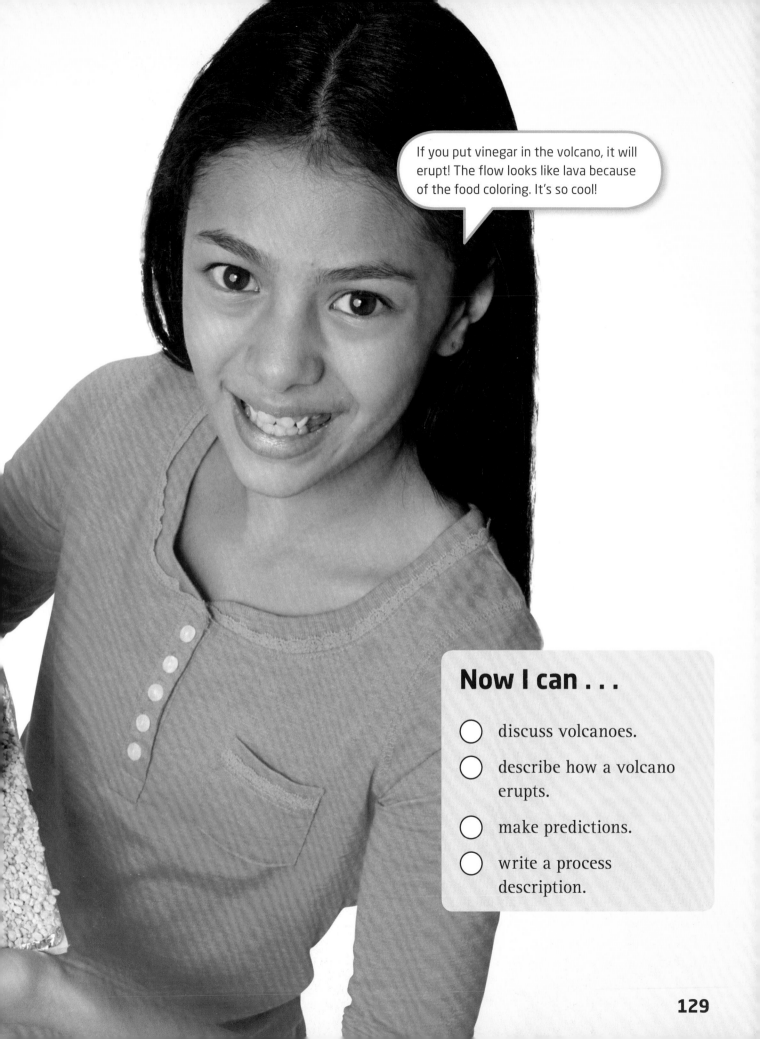

If you put vinegar in the volcano, it will erupt! The flow looks like lava because of the food coloring. It's so cool!

Now I can . . .

○ discuss volcanoes.

○ describe how a volcano erupts.

○ make predictions.

○ write a process description.

Reduce,
Reuse,
Recycle

Starry Night, Jane Perkins

In this unit, I will . . .
- discuss the importance of reducing, reusing, and recycling.
- learn about art from recycled materials.
- talk about what I can do to help the environment.
- write a biography.

Check T for *True* and F for *False*.

1. This is a painting.   **T** **F**

2. This is made from trash.   **T** **F**

3. This is a landfill.   **T** **F**

4. This is a toy.   **T** **F**

5. What would you make with recycled materials?

_____

VOCABULARY 1

1 **Listen and read.** TR: 8.1

2 **Listen and repeat.** TR: 8.2

Every day we make **trash.** Where does it go? Some of it is buried in **landfills.** Yuck! There has to be a better way. There is! You can choose a way of life that works with the **environment.** You can **conserve** instead of **throwing away.** You can make **energy-efficient** choices.

The three Rs of the environment are **reduce, reuse,** and **recycle.** We all know about recycling. **Man-made** things are crushed and melted down. They are then made into new things. The best Rs are to reduce and reuse. Reduce by choosing to use less energy. Reuse by finding new uses for **junk.**

Choosing **natural** materials is friendly to the environment. Things made from natural stuff are cool. When they are used up, just like other trash, they go into the landfill, too. But they break down faster. And natural things can be grown again. They're **renewable.**

Can we **design** things to reduce, reuse, and recycle? Yes! We can **build** houses that are energy efficient. We can make art with natural things, or reused things. The possibilities are endless.

3 **Ask and answer.** Work with a partner. What did you learn?

How can I conserve energy?

Turn off the lights when you aren't using them.

That's right! Reduce.

1 **Listen, read, and sing.** TR: 8.3

The Three Rs

When you're walking to the trash can
with some old stuff in your hand,
you might want to stop and think again.
Can this be reused or given away?
Let's start taking care of our world today!

CHORUS

Reduce. Reuse. Recycle.
Do it every day.
Don't throw everything into the trash
when clearly there's another way.

Reduce. Reuse. Recycle.
Help keep our world clean.
Do your part every day
to make our world green!

Recycling is easy when you know what to do.
Glass? Paper? Metal?
These things can be reused,
again, and again, and again!

CHORUS

Compost your uneaten food.
Composting isn't hard to do.
Natural things can be reused
when they get a helping hand from you!

Reduce. Reuse. Recycle.
Do it every day.
Don't throw everything into the trash
when clearly there's another way.

Reduce. Reuse. Recycle.
Help keep our world clean.
Reduce. Reuse. Recycle.
Help make our world green.

2 **Ask and answer.**
Work with a partner.

How do you recycle, reuse, or reduce?
- glass
- paper
- metal

Bruges, Belgium

GRAMMAR 1

Passive with modals (simple present) TR: 8.4

Natural things **can be grown** again.
Many things **can be made** into art!
Aluminum cans **must be melted** to be recycled.
Some plastics **may be put** in recycling containers.

1 **Read.** Complete the sentences.

1. Clothes (can/color) _____can be colored_____ with natural dyes.

2. Save the bricks that (can/reuse) _____, and the broken

   ones (can/throw away) _____.

3. Energy (may/conserve) _____ by making good choices.

4. Fleece sweaters (can/make) _____ from recycled

   water bottles.

5. Future cars (must/design) _____ to run on electricity.

6. A house (can/build) _____ with recycled materials.

2 **Write.** What things can be done to reduce, reuse, and recycle? Use the words in the list. Write sentences.

"green" shopping bags magazine water energy-efficient houses a faucet with a leak recycling centers	fix reuse build recycle conserve design

1. Water can be conserved. _____

2. _____

3. _____

4. _____

5. _____

6. _____

3 **Make sentences.** Work with a partner. Read one of your sentences. Your partner makes a sentence using the same verb. Take turns.

Water can be conserved.

Electricity can be conserved, too.

VOCABULARY 2

1 **Listen and repeat.**
Then read and write. TR: 8.5

chemicals

cardboard

metal

glass

tools

1. It is clear or colored. It can be melted down and reused. It is used to make bottles or windows. _____

2. It is made from paper. It is used to make shoe boxes. It is soft when wet.

   _____

3. They are used to clean things. They can hurt your skin. Don't drink them!

   _____

4. There are many kinds, and they have different uses. They help us do things that we can't do with just our hands. _____

5. This is used to make cans and also cars. It's used to make things that must be strong. _____

2 **Listen and stick.** TR: 8.6

1   2   3   4   5

GRAMMAR 2

Clauses with *when* TR: 8.7

When we recycle trash, we save on materials and energy.
An artist's work may surprise us **when we first see it.**

1 **Read and write.** How do you and your friends help the environment?
Use words in the box.

> bike   light   paper   plastic bottle   shopping bag   trash   water

1. When ___we leave the house___, ___we turn off the lights___.

2. _____ when _____.

3. When _____, _____.

4. When _____, _____.

5. _____ when _____.

2 **Play a game.** Cut out the spinner in the back of the book. Work in a
small group. Make sentences. Take turns.

When I go shopping,
I walk or go by bike.

I reuse a shopping bag
when I go shopping.

139

1 **Listen and read.** TR: 8.8

Recycling old aluminum cans into new ones uses 95% less energy than making new cans.

Found Art

We often think of reusing and recycling as something we just have to do. But some people see it as a chance to create. Any object can be reused to make something amazing. Reusing is more than a way to save—it can help us think about things in new and different ways.

Using found stuff to make art is not new. *Found art* became popular in the 1900s. Found art made people think about the things around them in a different way. Many things could be made into art!

Today many artists still make art from things they find. Sometimes they use things as they find them, and other times they make changes to the things they find. Sometimes they use junk. The trash from our homes has plenty of metal, plastic, rubber, and cardboard. Artists might use old toys, or objects they find on the beach, or old electrical equipment. The Korean artist, Yong Ho Ji, makes sculptures from old rubber tires. His sculptures are usually of realistic or imaginary animals. Brian Marshall, an American artist, makes sculptures of robots using objects he finds. The artists put it all together to express their thoughts. We can enjoy their creativity and be amazed at the artists' skill. We can also be surprised by our feelings. Often we can just appreciate the beauty or the humor. All these things make found art valuable in our lives.

Trash from home

Paper and cardboard **28.5%**

Food scraps **13.9%**

Yard waste **13.4%**

Plastics **12.4%**

Metal **9.0%**

Rubber, leather, and textiles **8.4%**

Wood **6.4%**

Glass **4.6%**

Other **3.4%**

Sculpture by Yong Ho Ji

2 Check T for *True* and F for *False*.

1. Using junk to make art is a way to reuse trash. (T) (F)

2. Found art always used trash. (T) (F)

3. Art made from junk is valuable because it makes us think in new ways. (T) (F)

4. Found art became popular in the 1850s. (T) (F)

5. Brian Marshall makes sculptures from rubber tires. (T) (F)

3 Label. Use these words.

fork
key
pencil sharpener
spoon

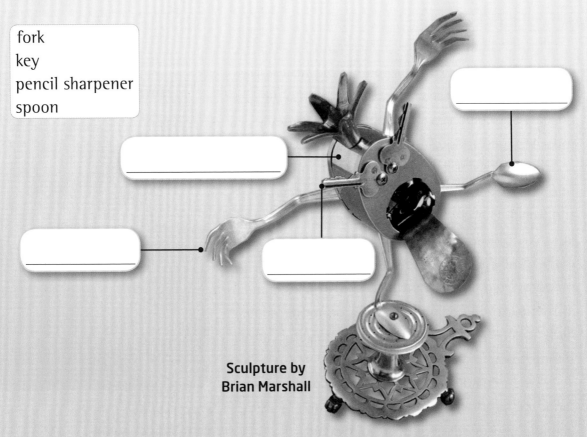

Sculpture by
Brian Marshall

4 Have a discussion. Work in a group. Look at these photos and the photo at the beginning of the unit. Discuss the art. Which do you like best? Explain why. Does your group agree?

5 Plan an art project. Work with a partner. Discuss creating trash art. What would you make, and what materials would you use?

WRITING

Biography A biography tells about the life and work of a person. You can include key dates, such as birth date, important events, and interesting facts in the person's life. You should also explain why this person is or was important. Use expressions such as *one of the most* and *the first*.

1 **Read.** Read about David Mach. Underline the facts that you find interesting. Why do you think he is important?

David Mach

David Mach was born in Scotland in 1956. He is an artist and is famous for his big sculptures that use many different kinds of objects. He has made sculptures from sports equipment, matches, and magazines.

His first exhibition was in London in 1982. He has now had exhibitions in many cities around the world. Some of his famous sculptures are in public places. He used old phone booths to make a sculpture on a street in London. He made a train out of bricks that is in the hills in the north of England. In 2012, he made some huge, colorful sculptures called Giants in a small Italian town.

Some of Mach's most famous sculptures are made of metal coat hangers. Some are of wild animals and another is of an astronaut.

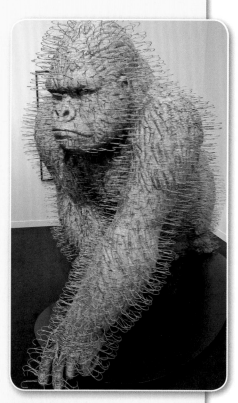

David Mach's coat-hanger gorilla

2 **Write.** Write about an important or interesting person. Include important details and dates from the person's life. Explain why he or she is important.

3 **Share.** Share your writing. Work in a small group. Listen and take notes.

Help reduce our human footprint.

Think. Pair. Share.

- What do you do to reduce, reuse, and recycle waste?

- What other things can your community do to reduce, reuse, and recycle waste?

- Compare your ideas with a partner or group. Decide which ideas are the best.

Earth at night

"People have created the problem, so it's critical to get the public excited and eager to participate in a solution."

Alexandra Cousteau, Water Advocate and Environmental Filmmaker, National Geographic Explorer

PROJECT

Make art from things you throw away.

1 Work in a small group. Collect different types of junk.

2 Look at your collected junk, and decide what to make.

3 Make your work of art.

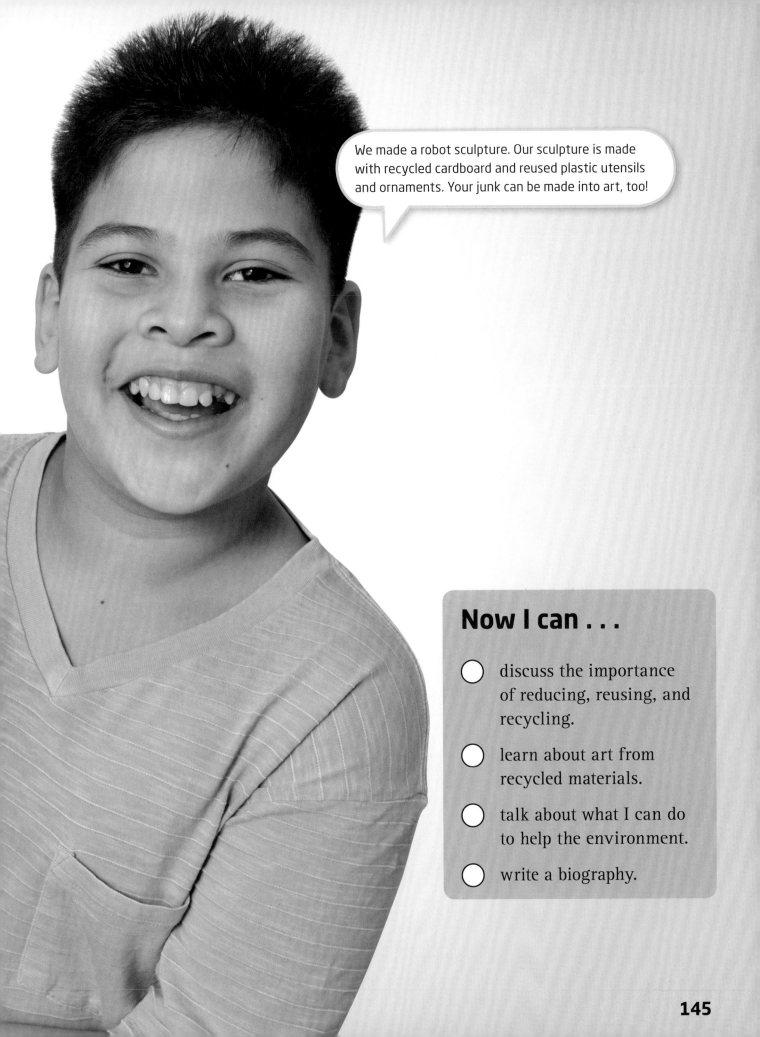

We made a robot sculpture. Our sculpture is made with recycled cardboard and reused plastic utensils and ornaments. Your junk can be made into art, too!

Now I can . . .

- ⚪ discuss the importance of reducing, reusing, and recycling.

- ⚪ learn about art from recycled materials.

- ⚪ talk about what I can do to help the environment.

- ⚪ write a biography.

Cool Vacations!

In this unit, I will . . .
- talk about different vacation places.
- talk about what I would do in different situations.
- express preferences.
- write a review.

Look and circle the correct letter.

1. What are the people doing?
   a. going on rides
   b. sliding down a water slide

2. Where are they?
   a. at an amusement park
   b. at a river

3. Would you like to go here? Why / Why not?

Santa Monica Pier, California, USA

VOCABULARY 1

1 **Listen and read.** TR: 9.1

2 **Listen and repeat.** TR: 9.2

Do you like vacations with lots of people and noise? Or places that are quiet with no people nearby? Let's find out about some cool vacations!

The whole family can enjoy **camping** together. Bring a **tent** and sleep in the fresh air. If you **hike** up a very big mountain, you have to take a **guide** to help you.

Do you like history? Go see the **ruins** of an old city. If you like the modern world, take a **tour** of a city! But if you like to learn how to protect the natural world, then an ecotour is for you!

Do you like animals and plants? Go on a **photo safari** and take pictures of **wildlife.** Stay safe in a truck when there are dangerous wild animals.

Santa Cruz, Peru

A resort is a good place to **relax** and have fun on your vacation. Stay the night at a big **hotel.** Go to the **beach** to sit in the sun and swim. Put on sunscreen so that your skin doesn't burn!

Theme parks are full of people having fun! Buy a **ticket** for an exciting ride, and hear people scream. If the theme park is also a **water park,** get ready to get wet!

camping

3 **Ask and answer.** Work with a partner. What did you learn?

What do you want to do on vacation?

I want to go camping!

1 **Listen, read, and sing.** TR: 9.3

If I Went on Vacation

CHORUS

Let's go on vacation!
Let's go on a trip!

If we went on vacation,
we would take a big ship
across the ocean,
far, far away.

If I had my way,
I would go today!

Camping and hiking!
The beach and the sun!
If we went on vacation,
it would be so much fun!

If we went on a tour,
we would see wildlife.
I would take lots of photos.
Wouldn't that be so nice?

CHORUS

I would like to stay at a hotel.
You'd like to relax.

Camping and hiking!
The beach and the sun!
If we went on vacation,
it would be so much fun!

If I weren't afraid of heights,
we could climb a mountain.
But I am! So let's go to the water park
and take pictures by the fountain.

CHORUS

Moremi Game Reserve, Botswana

2 **Work with a partner.**
Plan a vacation.

1. Where do you want to go? Why?
2. What will you bring with you?
3. What will you do there?

GRAMMAR 1

Second conditional TR: 9.4

If we **went** on a photo safari, I **would take** pictures of lions.
I'**d go** mountain climbing if I **weren't** afraid of heights.
He **wouldn't spend** all of his time in museums if he **didn't like** art.
If you **had** a lot of money, where **would** you **go** on vacation?

1 **Match.** Match the beginning of each sentence with the correct ending.

1. If I went to a theme park,
2. If I went to a big hotel at a resort,
3. If I visited an old city,
4. If I went on vacation in the mountains,
5. If I went on a photo safari,

a. I would enjoy seeing all the wild animals.
b. I would have fun on the rides.
c. I would bring a tent and go camping.
d. I would relax in the sun and go swimming.
e. I would take a tour of the ruins.

2 **Read and write.**

1. If I _____ (go) to Egypt, I _____ (visit) the

   Great Pyramid.

2. If we _____ (stay) at a hotel near the beach, we _____

   (go swim).

3. She _____ (go camp) if she _____ (have) a tent.

4. We _____ (learn) about the animals in this region if we

   _____ (take) an ecotour.

5. If the tour guide _____ (come) with us, she _____ (tell)

   us all about this place.

6. If he _____ (take) the train, he _____ (see) more

   of the country.

3 **Look and say.** Work with a partner. Look at the pictures and make sentences. Take turns.

If I went to the beach, I would go snorkeling.

I would go surfing if I went to the beach.

153

VOCABULARY 2

1 **Listen and repeat.**
Then read and write. TR: 9.5

a suitcase

sunglasses

a passport

souvenirs

an airport

1. When you travel to another country, you need a _____.

   It shows who you are and the country where you were born.

2. I always buy _____ when I'm on vacation. I like to look at

   them and remember the fun I had!

3. I don't like to carry a lot of stuff on vacation. I bring a small

   _____ for my clothes.

4. If we arrived at the _____ late, we would miss our plane.

5. Has anyone seen my _____? The snow is so bright in

   the sun.

2 **Listen and stick.** Do you think they had a good vacation? Why? TR: 9.6

1   2   3   4   5

GRAMMAR 2

Would rather TR: 9.7

I **would rather** go on an ecotour **than** go to a theme park.
We**'d rather** go on a tour **than** stay at the hotel.
He**'d rather** not eat at that restaurant.

1 **Make sentences.** Work with a partner. Take turns.

1. live by the ocean / in the mountains _____

_____

2. go camping / stay at a hotel _____

_____

3. ride a bike on a dirt path / motorcycle _____

_____

4. walk in the forest / city _____

_____

5. see wildlife on a photo safari / in the zoo _____

_____

6. wear sunscreen / get a sunburn _____

_____

2 **Play a game.** Cut out the board and the pictures in the back of the book. Choose nine pictures and put them in the spaces. Do not show your pictures. Work with a partner. Take turns.

B2. Let's go to a water park.

I don't feel like it. I'd rather go for a hike.

1 **Listen and read.** TR: 9.8

Tree House Vacation

Are you ready for a great eco-adventure? Have your vacation in a tree house! You can find them all over the world. Tree house vacations are in places such as Peru, Kenya, Belize, and India. There's a lot to do in nature!

In India, there are tree house bedrooms from 10 to 25 meters (35–80 feet) up a tree. There's a bamboo elevator to carry you up. It's powered by water! The electricity you use comes from the sun. And there are trails to hike and natural swimming pools to swim in. You can visit your neighbor by walking on a bridge made of rope!

You can stay in comfort at a tree house in Kenya. It has two floors, and the rooms have big beds. The windows have colored glass, and the bathrooms have showers. There's a small kitchen, too. The hotel serves food in your room! And if you get tired of living in nature, the city of Nairobi is about 30 minutes away.

In Belize, you can live with parrots under a Guanacaste tree that is about 30 meters (100 feet) tall. The parrots make good neighbors because they eat the insects! There are other birds, too. It's a great place for bird-watching. A river runs around the tree house on three sides. The clear water is good for swimming!

In Peru, you can stay in a bungalow, or a lodge, near the Yarapa River in the Amazon rain forest. The main lodge connects to the other 10 bungalows by passageways and steel cable bridges. One of the bungalows has a view of the Yarapa River. You can watch people fish in the river and you might even see a river dolphin. Sometimes you can see monkeys pass by your room as they look for food!

2 **Read.** Where are these tree houses? Write the location.

1. You can live with parrots in a tree house in _____.

2. You can vacation in comfort in a tree house in _____.

3. You might see monkeys looking for food in _____.

4. A bamboo elevator carries you to your tree house in _____.

3 **Listen and write.** Work with a partner. Compare places for a tree house vacation. Your partner will listen and complete the first two rows. Then listen to your partner, and fill in the last two rows.

Watching wildlife	
Living in comfort	
Walking on tree bridges	
Using power from nature	

4 **Rank the vacations.** Places for a vacation. Rank the vacations in order of preference (1 = most favorite). Work with a partner. Compare and explain your choices.

Rank	Vacations	Why you want to go there
	Ice hotel	
	Underwater hotel	
	Sports camp	
	Martial arts camp	
	Make-a-movie camp	
	Astronaut camp	
	Tree house	

A company is planning future vacations on the moon! Some tourists have already visited the space station. But it's expensive!

Iquitos, Peru

157

WRITING

Travel Review A travel review describes someone's experience of a vacation. Based on your review, another person can decide if they want to do the same vacation. To make your writing interesting, you can use different kinds of sentences. You can use short, simple sentences to describe your ideas. Or you can combine your ideas into longer sentences. You can also use questions or exclamations.

1 **Read.** Read the ecotour review. Underline an example of a sentence that describes just one idea, and circle another that describes more than one idea.

Review of the Antigua Ecotour

If you wanted a special vacation on a beautiful island, where would you go? I recommend this ecotour in Antigua.

The tour guides took our small group on a boat to a natural rock bridge called Hell's Gate. We had to swim to the island and walk up the rocks and through a cave. Then we walked across the bridge. The view from the top was spectacular! The guides give you a tasty lunch on the boat and then it's time to go snorkeling! The boat stopped at a coral reef and we explored the wildlife. We saw many colorful fish. We saw a stingray, too! The water can be rough, so snorkeling is hard work. But it's worth the effort. When we got back on the boat, there was a snack of banana bread ready for us. Delicious!

If you prefer doing something active on vacation instead of sitting on the beach, this is the trip for you!

coral reef

stingray

2 **Write.** Write a review of a vacation. Tell what you liked and didn't like. Describe what you saw and did. Remember to use different types of sentences.

3 **Share.** Share your writing. Work in a small group. Listen and take notes.

Be a respectful tourist.

Think. Pair. Share.

- Is tourism a good thing for a place? Is it a good thing for local people?

- How should tourists show respect for the places they visit?

- Compare your ideas with a partner or group. Which ideas does everyone like best?

Singapore

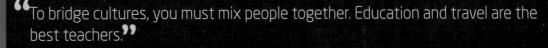

"To bridge cultures, you must mix people together. Education and travel are the best teachers."

Joseph Lekuton Teacher, National Geographic Explorer

PROJECT

Make a tourist brochure.

1 Work with a partner. Choose an interesting place in your country.

2 Research the place. What can you do there? What places can you visit?

3 Make a brochure with pictures and text.

Colonia [del Sacramento], Uruguay

Colonia was founded by the Portuguese in 1680 on the Río de la Plata.

The lighthouse was built in 1857 over the ruins of a convent. You can go to the top and see the views.

You can see Portuguese and Spanish architecture.

Map of Colonia del Sacramento

Río de la Plata

Museo Español

Plaza de Agosto

Plaza de Armas

Plaza Mayor

Río de la Plata

Bastión de San Miguel

There's a lot to do in Colonia. You should visit the lighthouse and the museums!

Now I can . . .

- ⭕ talk about different vacation places.

- ⭕ talk about what I would do in different situations.

- ⭕ express preferences.

- ⭕ write a review.

Review

1 **Read.** Complete these sentences. Use each word only once. Then make similar sentences about yourself.

> because   could   when   will   would

1. I couldn't go to the water park _____ of the rain.

2. If I have time, I _____ go to the new theme park.

3. A lot of junk _____ be made into art.

4. I _____ run away if a volcano erupted!

5. Some parts of our brain become active _____ we look at art.

2 **Work with a partner.** Talk about your dream vacation.

> if / will
> if / would
> would rather

> If my parents say yes, we will go on a photo safari!

> I would rather go to a water park!

> And if I didn't have to come to school, I would travel around the world for six months.

3 **Role-play.** Work with a partner. Practice and perform for the class.

Student A:
You are a scientist who studies volcanoes. Answer the reporter's questions.

Student B:
You are a student interviewing the scientist for the school magazine. Ask questions.

> ash   dormant   erupt   extinct   heat   steam
> crater   environment   eruption   gas   lava   volcano

> Are dormant volcanoes dangerous?

> Yes, sometimes they become active.

4 **Write.** Work with a partner. Look at the photo. How can these things be reused?

1. Old cans can be _____.

2. _____.

3. _____.

4. _____.

5 **Listen to the ads.** Check the mini-vacation. TR: 9.9

	Photo safari	Ecotour
Visit exotic places near your home.		
Get to know your own city.		
Bring a tent and a sleeping bag.		
Make art.		
Get up early on Sunday.		
Bring just a sleeping bag.		
Take pictures at the recycling center.		

6 **Ask and answer.** Work with a partner.

1. What will you do this weekend if you have free time?
2. Of the two weekend tours in activity 5, which would you rather do? Why?
3. If you could travel for six months, where would you go?

7 **Work in small groups.** Create a brochure for a weekend trip near your city.

camping	guide	junk	relax	suitcase	tent	ticket
environment	hike	natural	ruins	sunglasses	theme park	tour

1 **Listen and read.** TR: 9.10

Surviving Krakatoa

My sister and I were lucky. We survived the tsunami that came after Krakatoa erupted in 1883. Many people didn't live. Let me tell you what happened.

Our house was high on a hill above the town of Anjer. My little sister, Melati, didn't like this because whenever we had to go into town, we had to walk a long way. I liked the walk down into Anjer. I could look across the sea. Often I could see the volcano on Krakatoa Island.

Melati and I were visiting our cousins in Anjer but something was wrong. We heard eruptions from Krakatoa. They were as loud as a hundred thunder claps. We could see bright lights through the dark smoke on top of the volcano. It was Sunday night and I wanted to go home.

"I've never seen anything like this," said Auntie. "If you stay here, you'll be safe."

When we woke up the next morning, we couldn't see the sun. At 10 o'clock it was still dark. Everything was covered in ashes.

"Mom and Dad are going to be worried. We have to go home," I told Melati.

"No. Something bad might happen," she said.

I took her hand and pulled her up the path. We couldn't see much. We climbed as fast as we could. Suddenly, there was a strange calm. Then a wall of water roared over Anjer.

"A tsunami! Run Melati!" I shouted.

We ran. We heard horrible crashing but we didn't look back.

It went silent again. Then we heard another roar. A bigger tsunami rushed up the hill toward us.

"Melati! Darma! Take our hands!" It was Mom and Dad. They dragged us up to the house as the water raged beneath us. We were safe.

It was dark for many days after that. We were scared and hungry but we were alive. Anjer was flooded. The tsunami destroyed everything—houses, trees, people. We never found Auntie and my cousins.

Most of the volcano on Krakatoa was destroyed. And I could no longer see it when I looked across the sea.

2 **Read.** Check T for *True* and F for *False*.

1. Darma is telling the story.   (T) (F)

2. Melati and Darma slept at their aunt's house.   (T) (F)

3. Melati and Darma's aunt survived the tsunami.   (T) (F)

4. A hurricane caused the tsunami.   (T) (F)

3 **Read.** With a partner, put the items in order.

_____ There was a strange silence.

_____ They woke up but everything was dark and there were ashes everywhere.

_____ Their parents found them.

_____ They left the town and started climbing the hill.

__1__ There was smoke and light above Krakatoa. They heard loud explosions.

_____ The first tsunami covered the town.

4 **Express yourself.** Choose an activity.

1. After the tsunami, Darma's family faced many problems. Imagine you are a news reporter. Interview the family and write about the family's day after the tsunami.

2. Krakatoa re-erupted not long ago. Find another example of a recent volcanic eruption. Do a short presentation for the class.

3. Imagine that you are Melati. Retell the story from Melati's point of view.

Krakatoa Island, Indonesia

No way!

I will . . .
- agree and disagree.
- discuss possibilities.
- ask for opinions.

1 **Listen and read.** TR: 9.11

Maria: Are there any good movies showing tonight, Carla?
Carla: Well, there's a comedy. **What do you think,** guys?
Ivana: **No way!** Comedies are silly. **What else is there?**
Carla: Um, there's an action film. **What do you think?**
Ivana: Yes! Action films are the best!
Carla: **I suppose so.** But sometimes they are too violent.
Maria: **Exactly!** Isn't there anything else?

What do you think?	No way!	What else is there?	I suppose so.
How about _____?	Definitely not!	Is(n't) there anything else?	I guess so.
		Anything else?	Maybe.
	Exactly!	Do you have any other ideas?	Possibly.
	Right!		
	Totally!		
	Yeah, I agree.		
	Definitely!		

2 **Discuss.** Work in groups of three. Use the chart. Talk about what to do this weekend.

Our presentation is about . . .

I will . . .
- introduce ourselves.
- explain what our presentation is about.
- check with the audience.
- get started.

3 **Listen and read.** TR: 9.12

Gaby: **Hello, everyone. I'm** Gaby, and **this is** Berto.
Berto: **Our presentation is about** vacations.
Gaby: **Today we're going to show you** our vacation brochure.
Berto: **Our talk has two parts.** So **I'll start,** and then Gaby **will continue.**
Gaby: **Can everyone see?**
Students: Yes!
Berto: Great. **Let's start.**

Hello (everyone). Good morning. Good afternoon, everyone.	I'm _____. This is _____. My name's _____. I'd like to present _____.	Our presentation/ project is about . . . Our talk compares _____ with _____. Today we're going to (show you / present) _____. Our talk has two parts.	Can everyone see/hear? Can you all see/hear?	Let's start. Let's get started. I'll start/ begin. _____ will continue.

4 **Listen.** Circle the object that students present in each discussion. TR: 9.13

1. Mia and Ivan are presenting   a. a brochure.   b. an invention.   c. a poster.

2. Sonia and Juan are presenting   a. a brochure.   b. an invention.   c. a poster.

5 **Work in pairs.** Prepare and practice presentations.

1. Show the class a brochure you made for your project.

2. Present an invention you created.

3. Show the class a poster you made.

Irregular Verbs

Infinitive	Simple Past	Past Participle	Infinitive	Simple Past	Past Participle
be	was/were	been	light	lit	lit
beat	beat	beaten	lose	lost	lost
become	became	become	make	made	made
begin	began	begun	meet	met	met
bend	bent	bent	pay	paid	paid
bite	bit	bitten	put	put	put
bleed	bled	bled	read	read	read
blow	blew	blown	ride	rode	ridden
break	broke	broken	ring	rang	rung
bring	brought	brought	rise	rose	risen
build	built	built	run	ran	run
buy	bought	bought	say	said	said
catch	caught	caught	see	saw	seen
choose	chose	chosen	sell	sold	sold
come	came	come	send	sent	sent
cost	cost	cost	set	set	set
cut	cut	cut	sew	sewed	sewn
dig	dug	dug	shake	shook	shaken
do	did	done	shine	shone	shone
draw	drew	drawn	show	showed	shown
drink	drank	drunk	shut	shut	shut
drive	drove	driven	sing	sang	sung
eat	ate	eaten	sink	sank	sunk
fall	fell	fallen	sit	sat	sat
feed	fed	fed	sleep	slept	slept
feel	felt	felt	slide	slid	slid
fight	fought	fought	speak	spoke	spoken
find	found	found	spend	spent	spent
fly	flew	flown	spin	spun	spun
forget	forgot	forgotten	stand	stood	stood
forgive	forgave	forgiven	steal	stole	stolen
freeze	froze	frozen	stick	stuck	stuck
get	got	gotten	sting	stung	stung
give	gave	given	stink	stank	stunk
go	went	gone	sweep	swept	swept
grow	grew	grown	swim	swam	swum
hang	hung	hung	swing	swung	swung
have	had	had	take	took	taken
hear	heard	heard	teach	taught	taught
hide	hid	hidden	tear	tore	torn
hit	hit	hit	tell	told	told
hold	held	held	think	thought	thought
hurt	hurt	hurt	throw	threw	thrown
keep	kept	kept	understand	understood	understood
know	knew	known	wake up	woke up	woken up
leave	left	left	wear	wore	worn
lend	lent	lent	win	won	won
let	let	let	write	wrote	written
lie	lay	lain			

isn't it?	is it?	aren't they?	are they?
don't they?	do they?	doesn't it?	does it?
were they?	weren't they?	did it?	didn't it?

anyone

everyone

no one

someone

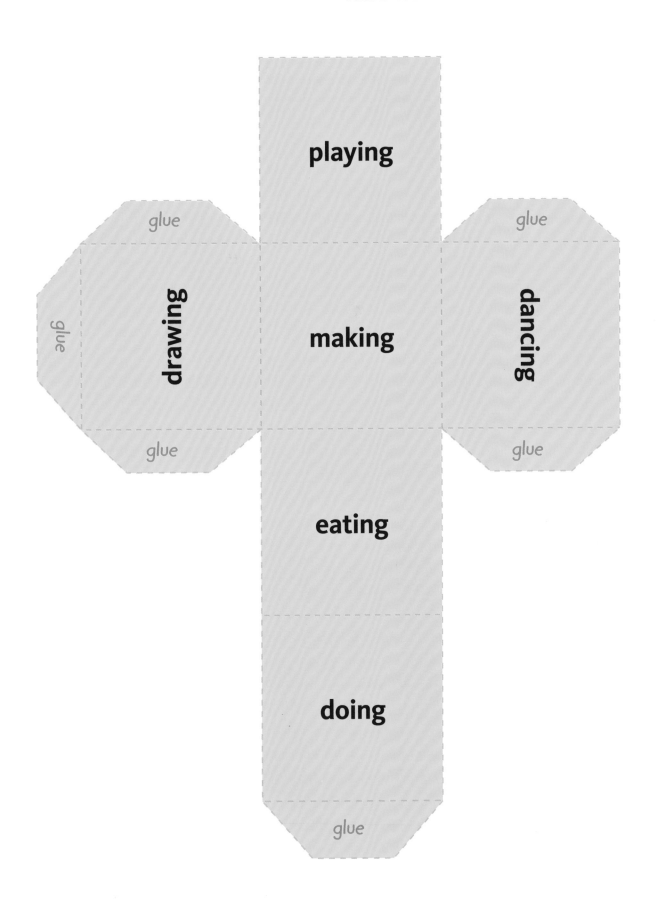

eruption

cold weather

steam

active volcano

hurricane

ash

lava

heat

rain

snow

sandstorm

tornado

flood

blizzard

heat wave

drought

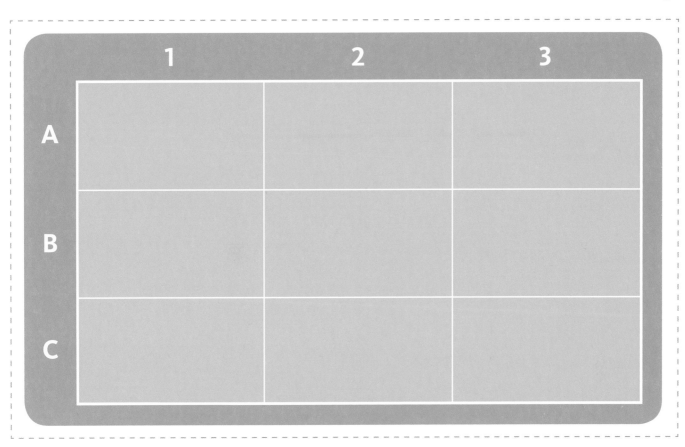

A water park

Horseback riding

Whitewater rafting

Sight seeing

A photo safari

Camping

Playing tennis

Eating in a restaurant

Visiting a science or natural history museum

A visit to an aquarium

Hiking on a mountain trail

A beach